FAVOURITE POEMS

101 CHILDREN'S CLASSICS

Scholastic Children's Books
An imprint of Scholastic Ltd
Euston House, 24 Eversholt Street, London, NW1 1DB, UK
Registered office: Westfield Road, Southam,
Warwickshire, CV47 0RA
SCHOLASTIC and associated logos are trademarks and/or
registered trademarks of Scholastic Inc.

First published in the UK by Scholastic Ltd, 2016

Introduction, poem notes and glossary copyright ©
Scholastic Ltd., 2016

ISBN 978 1407 16243 0

A CIP catalogue record for this book
is available from the British Library.

Printed by CPI Group (UK) Ltd, Croydon, CR0 4YY

Papers used by Scholastic Children's Books are made
from wood grown in sustainable forests

1 3 5 7 9 10 8 6 4 2

www.scholastic.co.uk

FAVOURITE POEMS

101 CHILDREN'S CLASSICS

INTRODUCTION

What makes a poem a classic? We believe it's the ones that stick in the mind long after reading. The ones that capture a thought or feeling with jewel-like perfection. The ones that reveal their meaning layer after layer over time.

Some of these classics have been around for centuries and speak of a distant past – of ancient kings and queens, brave knights, legendary monsters. Some speak of modern life, its joys and challenges. Many are from close to home – the familiar shown to us in unexpected ways – while others are from faraway lands. Their themes are universal though: the things we find fun, painful, beautiful; things that we love or are scared of.

And, of course, there is nonsense too – plenty of this!

All the most famous names are here – Tennyson, Keats, Shelley, Wordsworth, Edward Lear, Emily Dickinson, Christina Rossetti, William Shakespeare – along with some that may be new or surprising: Willis Wallis, writer of "Swing Low, Sweet Chariot", James Lord Pierpont, who penned "Jingle Bells", and Queen Elizabeth I – who found time to pen memorable poems while ruling Tudor England – among many more.

Also included are traditional rhymes, riddles, carols and songs, many of which will be familiar, and all of which have earned themselves a special place in our hearts.

So, whether you are discovering these wonderful poems for the first time, or rediscovering verses you already knew, we hope you enjoy the journey!

Scholastic Children's Books

CONTENTS

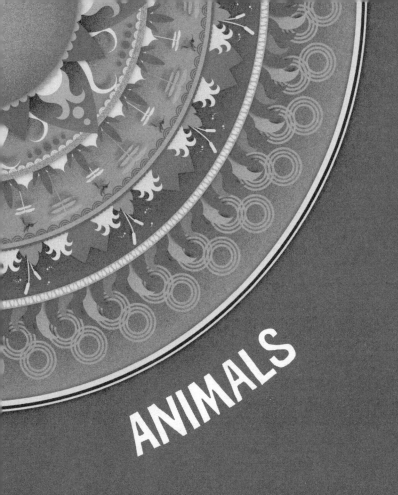

ANIMALS

The Tyger

William Blake (1757–1827)

William Blake was a poet, painter and engraver. His poems are often full of powerful images. Which images grab your attention in "The Tyger"? The poem depicts God as a blacksmith, forging the tiger. What doubt or confusion does he express about God's creation?

Tyger! Tyger! burning bright
In the forests of the night,
What immortal hand or eye
Could frame thy fearful symmetry?

In what distant deeps or skies
Burnt the fire of thine eyes?
On what wings dare he aspire?
What the hand, dare seize the fire?

And what shoulder, & what art,
Could twist the sinews of thy heart?
And when thy heart began to beat,
What dread hand? & what dread feet?

What the hammer? what the chain,
In what furnace was thy brain?
What the anvil? what dread grasp
Dare its deadly terrors clasp!

When the stars threw down their spears,
And water'd heaven with their tears,
Did he smile his work to see?
Did he who made the Lamb make thee?

Tyger! Tyger! burning bright
In the forests of the night,
What immortal hand or eye
Dare frame thy fearful symmetry?

An Old Silent Pond

Basho Matsuo (1644–1694)

This famous poem by Japanese poet Basho Matsuo is a "haiku". A typical haiku is a three-line poem that observes a moment. A haiku has a fixed number of syllables per line. Can you work out the pattern? With so few words, each one must have a strong impact. In this example, are the words effective in conjuring the scene?

An old silent pond.
A frog jumps into the pond,
splash! Silence again.

Little Fish

D. H. Lawrence (1885–1930)

D. H. Lawrence was a writer, poet and playwright working in the early twentieth century. Much of his writing explores the vitality of life. Look at the adjectives Lawrence uses to describe the fish. Are they effective in bringing the subject to life? Why do you think Lawrence made the poem so short?

> The tiny little fish enjoy themselves
> in the sea.
> Quick little splinters of life,
> their little lives are fun to them
> in the sea.

To a Mouse

*On Turning Her up in Her Nest with
the Plough, November, 1785*

Robert Burns (1759–1796)

As a farmer, Robert Burns was expected to kill pests like mice.
Instead, this poem shows his humanity and love of all creatures.
The poem's speaker addresses the mouse as if it were person. What
language does Burns use to give the mouse thoughts and feelings?
Try reading the poem aloud – the unusual spellings may seem much
easier to decipher!

Wee, sleekit, cow'rin, tim'rous beastie,
O, what a panic's in thy breastie!
Thou need na start awa sae hasty,
            Wi' bickering brattle!
I wad be laith to rin an' chase thee,
            Wi' murd'ring pattle!

I'm truly sorry man's dominion
Has broken Nature's social union,
An' justifies that ill opinion
            Which makes thee startle
At me, thy poor earth-born companion
            An' fellow-mortal!

I doubt na, whiles, but thou may thieve;
What then? poor beastie, thou maun live!
A daimen icker in a thrave
                    'S a sma' request;
I'll get a blessin wi' the lave,
                    And never miss't!

Thy wee bit housie, too, in ruin!
Its silly wa's the win's are strewin!
An' naething, now, to big a new ane,
                    O' foggage green!
An' bleak December's winds ensuin,
                    Baith snell an' keen!

Thou saw the fields laid bare and waste,
An' weary winter comin fast,
An' cozie here, beneath the blast,
                    Thou thought to dwell,
Till crash! the cruel coulter past
                    Out thro' thy cell.

That wee bit heap o' leaves an' stibble
Has cost thee mony a weary nibble!
Now thou's turned out, for a' thy trouble,
                    But house or hald,
To thole the winter's sleety dribble,
                    An' cranreuch cauld!

But, Mousie, thou art no thy lane,
In proving foresight may be vain:
The best laid schemes o' mice an' men
                    Gang aft a-gley,
An' lea'e us nought but grief an' pain,
                    For promised joy.

Still thou are blest, compared wi' me!
The present only toucheth thee:
But och! I backward cast my e'e,
                    On prospects drear!
An' forward, tho' I canna see,
                    I guess an' fear!

The Caterpillar

Christina Rossetti (1830–1894)

Christina Rossetti was one of the best-known female poets of the nineteenth century. "The Caterpillar" uses simple, clear language that seems to reflect the single-mindedness of the small creature. What is the caterpillar's mission? There is a single use of metaphor in this poem. Can you find it and does it enhance the poem's impact?

Brown and furry
Caterpillar in a hurry,
take your walk
To the shady leaf, or stalk,
Or what not,
Which may be the chosen spot.
No toad to spy you,
Hovering bird of prey pass by you;
Spin and die,
To live again a butterfly.

The Fly

William Blake (1757–1827)

"The Fly" comes from William Blake's collection *Songs of Experience*. Blake was keen to explore both the joy and suffering in human existence. Why do you think he chooses to draw a comparison between a fly and a human? What do you think the "blind hand" in the third stanza refers to?

Little fly,
Thy summer's play
My thoughtless hand
Has brush'd away.

Am not I
A fly like thee?
Or art not thou
A man like me?

For I dance,
And drink, & sing;
Till some blind hand
Shall brush my wing.

If thought is life
And strength & breath;
And the want
Of thought is death;

Then am I
A happy fly,
If I live,
Or if I die!

The Grey Squirrel

Humbert Wolfe (1885–1940)

Humbert Wolfe was an Italian-born British poet, whose work was particularly popular in the 1920s. Grey squirrels are common pests because of the threat they pose to their red relatives. Wolfe uses enjambment (running a sentence across a line break) at the end of the first and third stanzas. What is the impact of this technique on the way the poem is read?

Like a small grey
coffee-pot,
sits the squirrel.
He is not

all he should be,
kills by dozens
trees, and eats
his red-brown cousins.

The keeper on the
other hand,
who shot him, is
a Christian, and

loves his enemies,
which shows
the squirrel was not
one of those.

The Eagle
Fragment

Alfred, Lord Tennyson (1809–1892)

Alfred, Lord Tennyson was an eminent Victorian poet. He served as Poet Laureate from 1850 until 1892, and was the first writer to be awarded a peerage. "The Eagle" describes a bird of prey looking over the landscape. Why do you think Tennyson avoids using the bird's name? Alliteration is the technique of using words that begin with the same letter. Can you spot its use in this poem?

He clasps the crag with crooked hands;
Close to the sun in lonely lands,
Ring'd with the azure world, he stands.

The wrinkled sea beneath him crawls;
He watches from his mountain walls,
And like a thunderbolt he falls.

Robin Redbreast

William Allingham (1824–1889)

William Allingham was an Irish poet who often wrote about nature or fairies. This poem uses the robin to symbolize autumn. The poem's style could be described as sentimental – it aims to pull on the reader's heart strings! What language does the poem use to make us empathize with the robin?

Goodbye, goodbye to Summer!
    For Summer's nearly done;
The garden smiling faintly,
    Cool breezes in the sun;
Our Thrushes now are silent,
    Our Swallows flown away—
But Robin's here, in coat of brown,
    With ruddy breast-knot gay.
Robin, Robin Redbreast,
    O Robin dear!
Robin singing sweetly
    In the falling of the year.

Bright yellow, red, and orange,
    The leaves come down in hosts;
The trees are Indian Princes,
    But soon they'll turn to Ghosts;
The scanty pears and apples

Hang russet on the bough,
It's Autumn, Autumn, Autumn late,
   'Twill soon be winter now.
Robin, Robin Redbreast,
   O Robin dear!
And welaway! my Robin,
   For pinching days are near.

The fireside for the Cricket,
   The wheatsack for the Mouse,
When trembling night-winds whistle
   And moan all round the house;
The frosty ways like iron,
   The branches plumed with snow—
Alas! in Winter, dead, and dark,
   Where can poor Robin go?
Robin, Robin Redbreast,
   O Robin dear!
And a crumb of bread for Robin,
   His little heart to cheer.

NATURE
AND LANDSCAPE

I Wandered Lonely as a Cloud

William Wordsworth (1770–1850)

William Wordsworth was one of the foremost Romantic poets. This poem was inspired by a walk he took with his sister Dorothy in the Lake District. He describes the daffodils like people "fluttering and dancing" (a technique called "personification"). How does this change how you think about daffodils?

I wandered lonely as a cloud
That floats on high o'er vales and hills,
When all at once I saw a crowd,
A host, of golden daffodils;
Beside the lake, beneath the trees,
Fluttering and dancing in the breeze.

Continuous as the stars that shine
And twinkle on the milky way,
They stretched in never-ending line
Along the margin of a bay:
Ten thousand saw I at a glance,
Tossing their heads in sprightly dance.

The waves beside them danced; but they
Outdid the sparkling waves in glee;
A poet could not but be gay,
In such a jocund company;
I gazed—and gazed—but little thought
What wealth the show to me had brought:

For oft, when on my couch I lie
In vacant or in pensive mood,
They flash upon that inward eye
Which is the bliss of solitude,
And then my heart with pleasure fills,
And dances with the daffodils.

Pleasant Sounds

John Clare (1793–1864)

This poem by John Clare is a "list poem". Each line represents a new item, or items, on the list of "pleasant sounds". What effect does the enumeration of images have? When a word sounds like the thing that it represents, it is said to be "onomatopoeic". Which onomatopoeic words can you find?

The rustling of leaves under the feet in woods and under
      hedges;
The crumpling of cat-ice and snow down wood-rides, narrow
      lanes, and every street causeway;
Rustling through a wood or rather rushing, while the wind
      halloos in the oak-top like thunder;
The rustle of birds' wings startled from their nests or flying
      unseen into the bushes;
The whizzing of larger birds overhead in a wood, such as
      crows, puddocks, buzzards;
The trample of robins and woodlarks on the brown leaves,
      and the patter of squirrels on the green moss;
The fall of an acorn on the ground, the pattering of nuts on
      the hazel branches as they fall from ripeness;
The flirt of the groundlark's wing from the stubbles – how
      sweet such pictures on dewy mornings, when the dew
      flashes from its brown feathers!

All Things Bright and Beautiful

Cecil Frances Alexander (1818–1895)

Cecil Frances Alexander was born in Ireland in 1818. This hymn may have been inspired by a verse from Samuel Taylor Coleridge's poem "The Rime of the Ancient Mariner": "He prayeth best, who loveth best; All things great and small; For the dear God who loveth us; He made and loveth all". What devices do you think make the poem so memorable?

All things bright and beautiful,
All creatures great and small,
All things wise and wonderful,
The Lord God made them all.

Each little flower that opens,
Each little bird that sings,
He made their glowing colours,
He made their tiny wings.

All things bright and beautiful,
All creatures great and small,
All things wise and wonderful,
The Lord God made them all.

The purple headed mountain,
The river running by,
The sunset and the morning,
That brightens up the sky.

All things bright and beautiful,
All creatures great and small,
All things wise and wonderful,
The Lord God made them all.

The cold wind in the winter,
The pleasant summer sun,
The ripe fruits in the garden,
He made them every one.

All things bright and beautiful,
All creatures great and small,
All things wise and wonderful,
The Lord God made them all.

The tall trees in the greenwood,
The meadows where we play,
The rushes by the water,
We gather every day.

All things bright and beautiful,
All creatures great and small,
All things wise and wonderful,
The Lord God made them all.

He gave us eyes to see them,
And lips that we might tell,
How great is God Almighty,
Who has made all things well.

Weathers

Thomas Hardy (1840–1928)

Thomas Hardy is a well-known British novelist and poet. He was
often inspired by the landscape of the south-west of England. What
are the two seasons depicted in "Weathers" and what images does
Hardy use to suggest them?

This is the weather the cuckoo likes,
    And so do I;
When showers betumble the chestnut spikes,
    And nestlings fly;
And the little brown nightingale bills his best,
And they sit outside at "The Traveller's Rest",
And maids come forth sprig-muslin drest,
And citizens dream of the south and west,
    And so do I.

This is the weather the shepherd shuns,
    And so do I;
When beeches drip in browns and duns,
    And thresh and ply;
And hill-hid tides throb, throe on throe,
And meadow rivulets overflow,
And drops on gate bars hang in a row,
And rooks in families homeward go,
    And so do I.

In the Darkened Fields

Mikiko Nakagawa (b. 1897)

Mikiko Nakagawa was a Japanese poet. This poem takes the form of a "tanka", a short unrhymed song of 31 syllables. The syllable structure of this poem is 5/7/5/7/7. The setting of tanka poetry is often an everyday scene. What do you think the simple images in this scene might also represent?

In the darkened fields
the very faintly burning
lights of the houses—
ah, they are more frail even
than the glowing of fireflies.

The Bluebell

Anne Brontë (1820–1849)

Anne Brontë was the youngest of the Brontë sisters, all of whom were famous novelists. In the nineteenth century, women often struggled to get their writing published, so many used male pseudonyms, including Anne, whose pen name was Acton Bell. In this poem different flowers have different effects on the speaker. How does the mood change when she sees the bluebell?

A fine and subtle spirit dwells
    In every little flower,
Each one its own sweet feeling breathes
    With more or less of power.

There is a silent eloquence
    In every wild bluebell
That fills my softened heart with bliss
    That words could never tell.

Yet I recall not long ago
    A bright and sunny day,
'Twas when I led a toilsome life
    So many leagues away;

That day along a sunny road
    All carelessly I strayed,
Between two banks where smiling flowers
    Their varied hues displayed.

Before me rose a lofty hill,
    Behind me lay the sea;
My heart was not so heavy then
    As it was wont to be.

Less harassed than at other times
    I saw the scene was fair,
And spoke and laughed to those around,
    As if I knew no care.

But when I looked upon the bank
    My wandering glances fell
Upon a little trembling flower,
    A single sweet bluebell.

Whence came that rising in my throat,
    That dimness in my eye?
Why did those burning drops distil,
    Those bitter feelings rise?

O, that lone flower recalled to me
    My happy childhood's hours
When bluebells seemed like fairy gifts
    A prize among the flowers.

Those sunny days of merriment
    When heart and soul were free,
And when I dwelt with kindred hearts
    That loved and cared for me.

I had not then mid heartless crowds
    To spend a thankless life
In seeking after others' weal
    With anxious toil and strife.

'Sad wanderer, weep those blissful times
    That never may return!'
The lovely floweret seemed to say,
    And thus it made me mourn.

Among the Rocks

Robert Browning (1812–1889)

Robert Browning is one of the most important poets of the nineteen century. In this poem, he celebrates being with nature, something that he felt was being lost as the cities expanded during the Industrial Revolution. Can you find examples of personification in this poem?

Oh, good gigantic smile o' the brown old earth,
　　This autumn morning! How he sets his bones
To bask i' the sun, and thrusts out knees and feet
　　For the ripple to run over in its mirth;
Listening the while, where on the heap of stones
　　The white breast of the sea-lark twitters sweet.

That is the doctrine, simple, ancient, true;
　　Such is life's trial, as old earth smiles and knows.
If you loved only what were worth your love,
　　Love were clear gain, and wholly well for you:
Make the low nature better by your throes!
　　Give earth yourself, go up for gain above!

Windy Nights

Robert Louis Stevenson (1850–1894)

Robert Louis Stevenson is skilled at bringing drama to subjects that at first glance seem quite ordinary. What do you notice about the relationship between the title and the content of the poem? Who do you think the galloping man might be?

Whenever the moon and stars are set,
    Whenever the wind is high,
All night long in the dark and wet,
    A man goes riding by.
Late in the night when the fires are out,
Why does he gallop and gallop about?

Whenever the trees are crying aloud,
    And the ships are tossed at sea,
By, on the highway, low and loud,
    By at the gallop goes he.
By at the gallop he goes, and then
By he comes back at the gallop again.

Composed Upon Westminster Bridge, September 3rd, 1802

William Wordsworth (1770–1850)

In this famous poem, William Wordsworth depicts the landscape of London, seen at dawn. The poem juxtaposes natural and urban imagery. What other techniques does Wordsworth use when describing the setting? Why do you think he chose to set the poem at dawn?

Earth has not anything to show more fair:
Dull would he be of soul who could pass by
A sight so touching in its majesty:
This City now doth, like a garment, wear
The beauty of the morning; silent, bare,
Ships, towers, domes, theatres, and temples lie
Open unto the fields, and to the sky;
All bright and glittering in the smokeless air.
Never did sun more beautifully steep
In his first splendour, valley, rock, or hill;
Ne'er saw I, never felt, a calm so deep!
The river glideth at his own sweet will:
Dear God! the very houses seem asleep;
And all that mighty heart is lying still!

MONTHS
AND SEASONS

Young Lambs

John Clare (1793–1864)

John Clare wrote many well-known poems about the English countryside. In this example he juxtaposes the freshness of spring with mortality: spring brings new life, but also a reminder of death. How does the ending change the tone of the poem?

The spring is coming by a many signs;
    The trays are up, the hedges broken down,
That fenced the haystack, and the remnant shines
    Like some old antique fragment weathered brown.
And where suns peep, in every sheltered place,
    The little early buttercups unfold
A glittering star or two—till many trace
    The edges of the blackthorn clumps in gold.
And then a little lamb bolts up behind
    The hill and wags his tail to meet the yoe,
And then another, sheltered from the wind,
    Lies all his length as dead—and lets me go
Close bye and never stirs but baking lies,
    With legs stretched out as though he could not rise.

Easter Wings

George Herbert (1593–1633)

George Herbert was a Welsh-born poet and clergyman. "Easter Wings" is an example of "concrete poetry", in which the subject is represented in the poem's shape. Key words and ideas are given extra emphasis by their position within the shape. Can you find examples of where the words work particularly well within the shape?

Lord, who createdst man in wealth and store,
Though foolishly he lost the same,
Decaying more and more
Till he became
Most poor:
With thee
O let me rise
As larks, harmoniously,
And sing this day thy victories:
Then shall the fall further the flight in me.

My tender age in sorrow did begin;
And still with sicknesses and shame.
Thou didst so punish sin,
That I became
Most thin.
With thee
Let me combine,
And feel this day thy victorie;
For, if I imp my wing on thine,
Affliction shall advance the flight in me.

Bed in Summer

Robert Louis Stevenson (1850–1894)

Robert Louis Stevenson was a Scottish poet and novelist. This poem comments on the changing daylight hours between summer and winter. As a child Stevenson was prone to sickness, and often had to spend days in bed. Does this autobiographical detail change the way you interpret the poem?

In winter I get up at night
And dress by yellow candle-light.
In summer, quite the other way,
I have to go to bed by day.

I have to go to bed and see
The birds still hopping on the tree,
Or hear the grown-up people's feet
Still going past me in the street.

And does it not seem hard to you,
When all the sky is clear and blue,
And I should like so much to play,
To have to go to bed by day?

Summer Shower

Emily Dickinson (1830–1886)

Emily Dickinson was an American poet. Her style is characterized by unusual syntax (word order) and clever imagery. Can you spot examples of both in this poem? Dickinson chooses to personify raindrops and the things that they encounter on their journey. How does it make you feel about the raindrops?

A drop fell on the apple tree,
Another on the roof;
A half a dozen kissed the eaves,
And made the gables laugh.

A few went out to help the brook,
That went to help the sea.
Myself conjectured, Were they pearls,
What necklaces could be!

The dust replaced in hoisted roads,
The birds jocoser sung;
The sunshine threw his hat away,
The orchards spangles hung.

The breezes brought dejected lutes,
And bathed them in the glee;
The East put out a single flag,
And signed the fete away.

To Autumn

John Keats (1795–1821)

John Keats was often inspired by nature and the seasons. In this poem he uses all the senses to describe the seasons. What representations of sight, touch, taste, smell and sound you can find? For Keats, autumn is a season of abundance, yet one that turns quickly to excess and decay. Can you find images that depict this?

Season of mists and mellow fruitfulness,
    Close bosom-friend of the maturing sun;
Conspiring with him how to load and bless
    With fruit the vines that round the thatch-eves run;
To bend with apples the moss'd cottage-trees,
    And fill all fruit with ripeness to the core;
        To swell the gourd, and plump the hazel shells
    With a sweet kernel; to set budding more,
And still more, later flowers for the bees,
Until they think warm days will never cease,
        For Summer has o'er-brimm'd their clammy cells.

Who hath not seen thee oft amid thy store?
    Sometimes whoever seeks abroad may find
Thee sitting careless on a granary floor,
    Thy hair soft-lifted by the winnowing wind;
Or on a half-reap'd furrow sound asleep,
    Drows'd with the fume of poppies, while thy hook

Spares the next swath and all its twined flowers:
And sometimes like a gleaner thou dost keep
    Steady thy laden head across a brook;
    Or by a cyder-press, with patient look,
       Thou watchest the last oozings hours by hours.

Where are the songs of Spring? Ay, where are they?
    Think not of them, thou hast thy music too—
While barréd clouds bloom the soft-dying day,
    And touch the stubble plains with rosy hue;
Then in a wailful choir the small gnats mourn
    Among the river sallows, borne aloft
       Or sinking as the light wind lives or dies;
And full-grown lambs loud bleat from hilly bourn;
    Hedge-crickets sing; and now with treble soft
The red-breast whistles from a garden-croft;
       And gathering swallows twitter in the skies

No!

Thomas Hood (1799–1845)

Thomas Hood was an English poet, known for his humorous verse. He opens this poem with a series of opposites to represent his subject. Do you find this technique successful? What effect does repetition have on the tone of the poem and do you agree with the speaker's feeling about the subject?

No sun – no moon!
No morn – no noon!
No dawn – no dusk – no proper time of day –
No sky – no earthly view –
No distance looking blue –
No road – no street – no "t'other side this way" –
No end to any Row –
No indications where the Crescents go –
No top to any steeple –
No recognitions of familiar people –
No courtesies for showing 'em –
No knowing 'em!
No travelling at all – no locomotion –
No inkling of the way – no notion –
"No go" by land or ocean –
No mail – no post –
No news from any foreign coast –
No Park, no Ring, no afternoon gentility –

No company – no nobility –
No warmth, no cheerfulness, no healthful ease,
No comfortable feel in any member –
No shade, no shine, no butterflies, no bees,
No fruits, no flowers, no leaves, no birds –
November!

'Twas the Night Before Christmas

Clement Clarke Moore (1779–1863)

Also known as "A Visit From St. Nicholas", this poem is traditionally read on Christmas Eve. Although it was originally published anonymously, Clement C. Moore later claimed authorship. Look at the language used to describe St Nicholas (or Father Christmas). Can you find examples of "similes" – the technique of describing something as being like something else?

'Twas the night before Christmas, when all through the house
Not a creature was stirring, not even a mouse;
The stockings were hung by the chimney with care,
In hopes that St. Nicholas soon would be there;

The children were nestled all snug in their beds;
While visions of sugar-plums danced in their heads;
And mamma in her 'kerchief, and I in my cap,
Had just settled our brains for a long winter's nap,

When out on the lawn there arose such a clatter,
I sprang from the bed to see what was the matter.
Away to the window I flew like a flash,
Tore open the shutters and threw up the sash.

The moon on the breast of the new-fallen snow,
Gave the lustre of mid-day to objects below,
When, what to my wondering eyes should appear,
But a miniature sleigh, and eight tiny reindeer,

With a little old driver, so lively and quick,
I knew in a moment it must be St Nick.
More rapid than eagles his coursers they came,
And he whistled, and shouted, and called them by name:

"Now Dasher! now, Dancer! now, Prancer and Vixen!
On, Comet! On, Cupid! on, Donder and Blitzen!
To the top of the porch! to the top of the wall!
Now dash away! dash away! dash away all!"

As dry leaves that before the wild hurricane fly,
When they meet with an obstacle, mount to the sky;
So up to the house-top the coursers they flew
With the sleigh full of Toys, and St. Nicholas too.

And then, in a twinkling, I heard on the roof
The prancing and pawing of each little hoof –
As I drew in my head, and was turning around,
Down the chimney St Nicholas came with a bound.

He was dressed all in fur, from his head to his foot,
And his clothes were all tarnished with ashes and soot;
A bundle of toys he had flung on his back,
And he looked like a pedlar, just opening his pack.

His eyes – how they twinkled; his dimples, how merry!
His cheeks were like roses, his nose like a cherry!
His droll little mouth was drawn up like a bow
And the beard of his chin was as white as the snow;

The stump of a pipe he held tight in his teeth,
And the smoke it encircled his head like a wreath;
He had a broad face and a little round belly,
That shook, when he laughed, like a bowlful of jelly.

He was chubby and plump, a right jolly old elf,
And I laughed when I saw him, in spite of myself;
A wink of his eye and a twist of his head
Soon gave me to know I had nothing to dread;

He spoke not a word, but went straight to his work,
And filled all the stockings; then turned with a jerk,
And laying his finger aside of his nose,
And giving a nod, up the chimney he rose;

He sprang to his sleigh, to his team gave a whistle,
And away they all flew like the down of a thistle,
But I heard him exclaim, ere he drove out of sight,
"Happy Christmas to all, and to all a good-night!"

Jingle Bells

James Lord Pierpoint (1822–1893)

"Jingle Bells" was first published with the title "One Horse Open Sleigh" in 1857 to celebrate Thanksgiving. The verse made history in December 1965 when they were the first song to be played in space. The lyrics of the original poem, below, differ slightly from those we know today. What differences can you spot? What does the rhythm of the poem make you think of?

Dashing through the snow
In a one-horse open sleigh
O'er the hills we go
Laughing all the way.
Bells on bobtail ring
Making spirits bright
Oh what sport to ride and sing
A sleighing song tonight!

Jingle bells, jingle bells,
Jingle all the way!
O what joy it is to ride
In a one-horse open sleigh.

A day or two ago
I thought I'd take a ride
And soon Miss Fannie Bright
Was seated by my side.
The horse was lean and lank
Misfortune seemed his lot
He got into a drifted bank
And the we got upsot.

Jingle bells, jingle bells,
Jingle all the way!
O what joy it is to ride
In a one-horse open sleigh.

A day or two ago
The story I must tell
I went out on the snow,
And on my back I fell;
A gent was riding by
In a one-horse open sleigh,
He laughed as there I sprawling lie,
But quickly drove away.

Jingle bells, jingle bells,
Jingle all the way!
O what joy it is to ride
In a one-horse open sleigh.

Now the ground is white
Go it while you're young,
Take the girls tonight
And sing this sleighing song;
Just get a bobtailed bay
Two forty is his speed
Hitch him to an open sleigh
And crack! You'll take the lead.

Jingle bells, jingle bells,
Jingle all the way!
O what joy it is to ride
In a one-horse open sleigh.

Over the Wintry

Natsume Sōseki (1867–1916)

Natsume Sōseki was a Japanese novelist and poet. He is so famous in Japan that his face used to be printed on the 1000-yen note. This poem is a haiku and uses personification to describe the wind. What emotional quality does this give to the poem?

Over the wintry
forest, winds howl in rage
with no leaves to blow.

In the Bleak Midwinter

Christina Rossetti (1830–1894)

Christina Rossetti wrote this story of the Nativity as a poem, but always intended for it to be sung aloud as a Christmas carol. Look at the rhyme scheme Rossetti uses. Why do you this poem makes a good song? How is the tone of the poem different from other Christmas carols you know?

In the bleak mid-winter
    Frosty wind made moan,
Earth stood hard as iron,
    Water like a stone;
Snow had fallen, snow on snow,
    Snow on snow,
In the bleak mid-winter
    Long ago.

Our God, Heaven cannot hold Him,
    Nor earth sustain;
Heaven and earth shall flee away
    When He comes to reign:
In the bleak mid-winter
    A stable-place sufficed
The Lord God Almighty
    Jesus Christ.

Enough for Him, whom cherubim
    Worship night and day,
A breastful of milk,
    And a mangerful of hay;
Enough for Him, whom angels
    Fall down before,
The ox and ass and camel
    Which adore.

Angels and archangels
    May have gathered there,
Cherubim and seraphim
    Thronged the air,
But only His mother
    In her maiden bliss
Worshipped the Beloved
    With a kiss.

What can I give Him,
    Poor as I am?
If I were a shepherd
    I would bring a lamb;
If I were a wise man
    I would do my part;
Yet what I can, I give Him,
    Give my heart.

Stopping by the Woods on a Snowy Evening

Robert Frost (1874–1963)

Robert Frost was born in San Francisco, USA, and his poetry often evokes the landscape of New England. In this poem, the speaker has trespassed onto someone else's land to watch the falling snow. Why do you think Frost makes a point of telling us so much about the man's other activities? Do you think the traveller would rather linger to enjoy the landscape?

Whose woods these are I think I know.
His house is in the village, though;
He will not see me stopping here
To watch his woods fill up with snow.

My little horse must think it queer
To stop without a farmhouse near
Between the woods and frozen lake
The darkest evening of the year.

He gives his harness bells a shake
To ask if there is some mistake.
The only other sound's the sweep
Of easy wind and downy flake.

The woods are lovely, dark and deep,
But I have promises to keep,
And miles to go before I sleep,
And miles to go before I sleep.

CHILDHOOD
AND OLD AGE

I Remember, I Remember

Thomas Hood (1799–1845)

Thomas Hood often wrote humorous or satirical poetry, but in this poem he is in a reflective mood, looking back nostalgically to his childhood. Nostalgia is a longing to return to the past. What images does Hood use to make the past seem welcoming? Does it remain welcoming throughout the poem?

I remember, I remember
    The house where I was born,
The little window where the sun
    Came peeping in at morn;
He never came a wink too soon
    Nor brought too long a day;
But now, I often wish the night
    Had borne my breath away.

I remember, I remember
    The roses red and white,
The violets and the lily cups—
    Those flowers made of light!
The lilacs where the robin built,
    And where my brother set
The laburnum on his birthday—
    The tree is living yet!

I remember, I remember
    Where I was used to swing,
And thought the air must rush as fresh
    To swallows on the wing;
My spirit flew in feathers then
    That is so heavy now,
The summer pools could hardly cool
    The fever on my brow.

I remember, I remember
    The fir-trees dark and high;
I used to think their slender tops
    Were close against the sky:
It was a childish ignorance,
    But now 'tis little joy
To know I'm farther off from Heaven
    Than when I was a boy.

When I Was One-and-Twenty
(from *A Shropshire Lad*)

A. E. Housman (1859–1936)

A. E. Housman's *A Shropshire Lad* is a collection of 63 poems, of which the poem below is the thirteenth. It describes advice given to a young man by another, wiser man. The advice is narrated in dialogue (words reported directly as if they were being spoken). What effect does this have? What do you think has happened to the young man?

When I was one-and-twenty
    I heard a wise man say,
"Give crowns and pounds and guineas
    But not your heart away;
Give pearls away and rubies
    But keep your fancy free."
But I was one-and-twenty,
    No use to talk to me.

When I was one-and-twenty
    I heard him say again,
"The heart out of the bosom
    Was never given in vain;
'Tis paid with sighs a plenty
    And sold for endless rue."
And I am two-and-twenty,
    And oh, 'tis true, 'tis true.

A Song About Myself

John Keats (1795–1821)

John Keats first trained as a medical student before deciding to become a professional poet. He is one of the most popular poets of the Romantic movement. This poem tells the tale of a young runaway. What does he find when he reaches his destination, and what do you think he is feeling when he gets here?

There was a naughty boy,
    A naughty boy was he,
He would not stop at home,
    He could not quiet be—
        He took
        In his knapsack
        A book
        Full of vowels
        And a shirt
        With some towels—
        A slight cap
        For night cap—
        A hair brush,
        Comb ditto,
        New stockings
        For old ones
        Would split O!
        This knapsack

Tight at's back
He rivetted close
And followéd his nose
To the north,
To the north,
And follow'd his nose
To the north.

There was a naughty boy
And a naughty boy was he,
For nothing would he do
But scribble poetry—
He took
An ink stand
In his hand
And a pen
Big as ten
In the other,
And away
In a pother
He ran
To the mountains
And fountains
And ghostes
And postes
And witches
And ditches
And wrote
In his coat
When the weather
Was cool,
Fear of gout,

And without
When the weather
Was warm—
Och the charm
When we choose
To follow one's nose
To the north,
To the north,
To follow one's nose
To the north!

There was a naughty boy
And a naughty boy was he,
He kept little fishes
In washing tubs three
In spite
Of the might
Of the maid
Nor afraid
Of his Granny-good—
He often would
Hurly burly
Get up early
And go
By hook or crook
To the brook
And bring home
Miller's thumb,
Tittlebat
Not over fat,
Minnows small
As the stall

Of a glove,
Not above
The size
Of a nice
Little baby's
Little fingers—
O he made
'Twas his trade
Of fish a pretty kettle
A kettle—
A kettle
Of fish a pretty kettle
A kettle!

There was a naughty boy,
    And a naughty boy was he,
He ran away to Scotland
    The people for to see—
        There he found
        That the ground
        Was as hard,
        That a yard
        Was as long,
        That a song
        Was as merry,
        That a cherry
        Was as red,
        That lead
        Was as weighty,
        That fourscore
        Was as eighty,
        That a door

Was as wooden
As in England—
So he stood in his shoes
And he wonder'd,
He wonder'd,
He stood in his shoes
And he wonder'd.

The Swing

Robert Louis Stevenson (1850–1894)

"The Swing", along with "From a Railway Carriage" and "Windy Nights", was published in Robert Louis Stevenson's collection *A Child's Garden of Verses*. What is the effect of the repetition of "up"? What do you think is going through the child's mind as he or she goes "up in the air and over the wall"?

How do you like to go up in a swing,
 Up in the air so blue?
Oh, I do think it the pleasantest thing
 Ever a child can do!

Up in the air and over the wall,
 Till I can see so wide,
River and trees and cattle and all
 Over the countryside—

Till I look down on the garden green,
 Down on the roof so brown—
Up in the air I go flying again,
 Up in the air and down!

Young and Old

Charles Kingsley (1819–1875)

Charles Kingsley was an English novelist, priest and poet. He was particularly interested in the "human condition": what it is to exist as a person. In this poem he writes about youth and old age. What imagery does he use to contrast the two? The two stanzas follow the same form and rhyme scheme. Why is this important?

When all the world is young, lad,
    And all the trees are green;
And every goose a swan, lad,
    And every lass a queen;
Then hey for boot and horse, lad,
    And round the world away;
Young blood must have its course, lad,
    And every dog his day.

When all the world is old, lad,
    And all the trees are brown;
When all the sport is stale, lad,
    And all the wheels run down;
Creep home, and take your place there,
    The spent and maimed among:
God grant you find one face there,
    You loved when all was young.

Mother's Song to a Baby

Anonymous

This poem is a traditional Native American lullaby. Can you see anything in the poem that suggests its heritage? How a poem is printed on the page can affect how we read it. What does the shape of this poem make you think of? Does it link to anything in the poem?

First
this little baby
has been given life
through the medicine man's song
through the medicine man's prayer
for this baby the songs
have been sung

Next
the baby's mother
has taken care of him
with the songs of the rain gods

This
little baby
in his cloud-cradle
was watched over by his mother

It
was
nice
how the clouds
came up like foam

And
as if he
was among them
this little baby
was cared for.

A Poet to His Baby Son

James Weldon Johnson (1871–1938)

James Weldon Johnson was an African–American poet, lawyer, diplomat and songwriter. He is best-known as leader of the National Association for the Advancement of Colored People, founded in 1909. In this poem, a new father worries for his young son's future. Do you think these same concerns apply today – and do you think the speaker truly believes his own advice?

Tiny bit of humanity,
Blessed with your mother's face,
And cursed with your father's mind.

I say cursed with your father's mind,
Because you can lie so long and so quietly on your back,
Playing with the dimpled big toe of your left foot,
And looking away,
Through the ceiling of the room, and beyond.
Can it be that already you are thinking of being a poet?

Why don't you kick and howl,
And make the neighbors talk about
"That damned baby next door,"
And make up your mind forthwith
To grow up and be a banker
Or a politician or some other sort of go-getter

Or—?—whatever you decide upon,
Rid yourself of these incipient thoughts
About being a poet.

For poets no longer are makers of songs,
Chanters of the gold and purple harvest,
Sayers of the glories of earth and sky,
Of the sweet pain of love
And the keen joy of living;
No longer dreamers of the essential dreams,
And interpreters of the eternal truth,
Through the eternal beauty.
Poets these days are unfortunate fellows.
Baffled in trying to say old things in a new way
Or new things in an old language,
They talk abracadabra
In an unknown tongue,
Each one fashioning for himself
A wordy world of shadow problems,
And as a self-imagined Atlas,
Struggling under it with puny legs and arms,
Groaning out incoherent complaints at his load.

My son, this is no time nor place for a poet;
Grow up and join the big, busy crowd
That scrambles for what it thinks it wants
Out of this old world which is—as it is—
And, probably, always will be.

Take the advice of a father who knows:
You cannot begin too young
Not to be a poet.

The First Tooth (excerpt)

Charles Lamb (1775–1834) and Mary Lamb (1764–1847)

Charles and Mary Lamb were siblings and literary collaborators, the authors of many well-known stories and poems for children. This poem is written from the perspective of a child. What is the key emotion that he or she is experiencing? What comparison words can you find in the poem?

Through the house what busy joy,
Just because the infant boy
Has a tiny tooth to show!
I have got a double row,
All as white, and all as small;
Yet no one cares for mine at all.
He can say but half a word,
Yet that single sound's preferred
To all the words that I can say
In the longest summer day.
He cannot walk, yet if he put
With mimic motion out his foot,
As if he thought he were advancing,
It's prized more than my best dancing.

Where Go the Boats

Robert Louis Stevenson (1850–1894)

Robert Louis Stevenson's poem is also written from the perspective
of a child. What game is the child playing? What does the final stanza
suggest will happen to the boats, and what do you think this change
might be a metaphor for?

Dark brown is the river,
Golden is the sand.
It flows along for ever,
With trees on either hand.

Green leaves a-floating,
Castles of the foam,
Boats of mine a-boating—
Where will all come home?

On goes the river,
And out past the mill,
Away down the valley,
Away down the hill.

Away down the river,
A hundred miles or more,
Other little children
Shall bring my boats ashore.

HISTORY,
LEGEND AND
HIGH ADVENTURE

The Song of Wandering Aengus

W. B. Yeats (1865–1939)

Yeats's poem tells the story of Aengus, a figure from Irish folklore.
Aengus is a god of love and poetry, often shown with birds circling
his head. Here he is described searching for a lost love. Have a look
at the images of nature at the beginning of the poem and at the end.
How do they change and why do you think this is?

I went out to the hazel wood,
Because a fire was in my head,
And cut and peeled a hazel wand,
And hooked a berry to a thread;
And when white moths were on the wing,
And moth-like stars were flickering out,
I dropped the berry in a stream
And caught a little silver trout.

When I had laid it on the floor
I went to blow the fire aflame,
But something rustled on the floor,
And someone called me by my name:
It had become a glimmering girl
With apple blossom in her hair
Who called me by my name and ran
And faded through the brightening air.

Though I am old with wandering
Through hollow lands and hilly lands,
I will find out where she has gone,
And kiss her lips and take her hands;
And walk among long dappled grass,
And pluck till time and times are done,
The silver apples of the moon,
The golden apples of the sun.

O Captain! My Captain!

Walt Whitman (1819–1892)

Walt Whitman was an American poet, and the subject of this famous poem is the US president Abraham Lincoln, who led his country through the American Civil War. The poem is an "extended metaphor poem": Lincoln is not represented directly but through a metaphor that continues throughout the poem. Whitman's opening lines express relief that the battle is won. How does he turn this tone of joy into one of grief?

O Captain! my Captain! our fearful trip is done;
The ship has weather'd every rack, the prize we sought is
      won;
The port is near, the bells I hear, the people all exulting,
While follow eyes the steady keel, the vessel grim and daring:
      But O heart! heart! heart!
        O the bleeding drops of red,
          Where on the deck my Captain lies,
          Fallen cold and dead.

O Captain! my Captain! rise up and hear the bells;
Rise up—for you the flag is flung—for you the bugle trills;
For you bouquets and ribbon'd wreaths—for you the shores
      a-crowding;
For you they call, the swaying mass, their eager faces turning;

Here Captain! dear father!
This arm beneath your head;
It is some dream that on the deck,
You've fallen cold and dead.

My Captain does not answer, his lips are pale and still;
My father does not feel my arm, he has no pulse nor will;
The ship is anchor'd safe and sound, its voyage closed and
done;
From fearful trip, the victor ship, comes in with object won;
Exult, O shores, and ring, O bells!
But I, with mournful tread,
Walk the deck my captain lies,
Fallen cold and dead.

A Life on the Ocean Wave

Epes Sargent (1813–1880)

Today, this poem is better known as a song: the official march of the US Merchant Marine Academy. Epes Sargent wrote it after watching the ships go out to sea from New York City harbour. The poem uses lots of similes. How do they help make life on the ocean seem glorious?

A life on the ocean wave,
A home on the rolling deep,
Where the scattered waters rave,
And the winds their revels keep!
Like an eagle caged, I pine
On this dull, unchanging shore:
Oh! give me the flashing brine,
The spray and the tempest's roar!

Once more on the deck I stand
Of my own swift-gliding craft:
Set sail! farewell to the land!
The gale follows fair abaft.
We shoot through the sparkling foam
Like an ocean-bird set free;—
Like the ocean-bird, our home
We'll find far out on the sea.

The land is no longer in view,
The clouds have begun to frown;
But with a stout vessel and crew,
We'll say, Let the storm come down!
And the song of our hearts shall be,
While the winds and the waters rave,
A home on the rolling sea!
A life on the ocean wave!

From a Railway Carriage

Robert Louis Stevenson (1850–1894)

Robert Louis Stevenson is most famous for his adventure novels, *Treasure Island* and *Kidnapped*, but many of his poems are about everyday subjects, brought to life with a vivid sense of adventure. What techniques does he use to bring a sense of excitement to a train journey?

Faster than fairies, faster than witches,
Bridges and houses, hedges and ditches;
And charging along like troops in a battle,
All through the meadows the horses and cattle:
All of the sights of the hill and the plain
Fly as thick as driving rain;
And ever again, in the wink of an eye,
Painted stations whistle by.
Here is a child who clambers and scrambles,
All by himself and gathering brambles;
Here is a tramp who stands and gazes;
And here is the green for stringing the daisies!
Here is a cart runaway in the road
Lumping along with man and load;
And here is a mill, and there is a river:
Each a glimpse and gone for ever!

Cockles and Mussels (or Molly Malone)

James Yorkston (dates unknown)

This song has been adopted as the unofficial anthem of Dublin –
though it is still not known whether or not Molly Malone was a real
historical character. Originally the verses were written by a Scotsman,
James Yorkston, to be sung in a music hall. The final verse and chorus
make use of irony: the refrain is no longer appropriate to the speaker.
What is the effect of this device on the reader?

In Dublin's fair city,
Where the girls are so pretty,
I first set my eyes upon Molly Malone.
She wheeled her wheelbarrow
Through the streets broad and narrow,
Singing, "cockles and muscles – alive, alive-o".

"Alive, alive-o,
Alive, alive-o."
Singing, "cockles and muscles,
Alive, alive-o."

She was a fishmonger,
And sure 'twas no wonder,
For so were her mother and father before.
They wheeled their wheelbarrows
Through the streets broad and narrow,

Singing, "cockles and muscles – alive, alive-o".

"Alive, alive-o,
Alive, alive-o."
Singing, "cockles and muscles,
Alive, alive-o."

She died of a fever,
And no one could save her,
And that was the end of sweet Molly Malone.
But her ghost wheels her barrow
Through the streets broad and narrow,
Singing, "cockles and muscles – alive, alive-o".

"Alive, alive-o,
Alive, alive-o."
Singing, "cockles and muscles,
Alive, alive-o."

"Alive, alive-o,
Alive, alive-o."
Singing, "cockles and muscles,
Alive, alive-o."

The Lady of Shalott (excerpt)

Alfred, Lord Tennyson (1809–1892)

"The Lady of Shalott" is a narrative poem that recounts one of the
Arthurian legends (medieval stories about the court of the legendary
King Arthur). This passage describes the moment when the Lady of
Shalott falls in love with Sir Lancelot then realizes she is cursed.
What literary devices does Tennyson use to create a sense of drama?

Part III
A bow-shot from her bower-eaves,
He rode between the barley-sheaves,
The sun came dazzling through the leaves,
And flamed upon the brazen greaves
    Of bold Sir Lancelot.
A red-cross knight for ever kneeled
To a lady in his shield,
That sparkled on the yellow field,
    Beside remote Shalott.

The gemmy bridle glittered free,
Like to some branch of stars we see
Hung in the golden Galaxy.
The bridle bells rang merrily
    As he rode down to Camelot:
And from his blazoned baldric slung
A mighty silver bugle hung,

And as he rode his armour rung,
     Beside remote Shalott.

All in the blue unclouded weather
Thick-jewelled shone the saddle-leather,
The helmet and the helmet-feather
Burned like one burning flame together,
     As he rode down to Camelot.
As often through the purple night,
Below the starry clusters bright,
Some bearded meteor, trailing light,
     Moves over still Shalott.

His broad clear brow in sunlight glowed;
On burnished hooves his war-horse trode;
From underneath his helmet flow'd
His coal-black curls as on he rode,
     As he rode down to Camelot.
From the bank and from the river
He flashed into the crystal mirror,
"Tirra lirra," by the river
     Sang Sir Lancelot.

She left the web, she left the loom,
She made three paces through the room,
She saw the water-lily bloom,
She saw the helmet and the plume,
     She look'd down to Camelot.
Out flew the web and floated wide;
The mirror cracked from side to side;
"The curse is come upon me," cried
     The Lady of Shalott.

Ozymandias

Percy Bysshe Shelley (1792–1822)

"Ozymandias" is another name for the Egyptian Pharaoh Ramesses II
(1303 BC–1213 BC). The poem was inspired by a statue in the British
Museum in London. Percy Shelley is one of the foremost Romantic
poets. One of the key ideas of Romantic poetry is that art remains
after death. How does the poem convey this idea?

I met a traveller from an antique land
Who said: Two vast and trunkless legs of stone
Stand in the desert. Near them on the sand,
Half sunk, a shattered visage lies, whose frown
And wrinkled lip and sneer of cold command
Tell that its sculptor well those passions read
Which yet survive, stamped on these lifeless things,
The hand that mocked them and the heart that fed.
And on the pedestal these words appear:
'My name is Ozymandias, King of Kings:
Look on my works, ye mighty, and despair!'
Nothing beside remains. Round the decay
Of that colossal wreck, boundless and bare,
The lone and level sands stretch far away.

Sir Gawain and the Green Knight (excerpt)

Anonymous

The author of this famous medieval narrative poem is unknown, but has been nicknamed the "Pearl Poet". Many medieval poets did not know how to write, but would perform their poems aloud. Their work would be passed from community to community, generation to generation, in what is called the "oral tradition".

The title character of the poem, Sir Gawain, is a knight in the legendary court of King Arthur. This excerpt tells the story of his encounter with the Green Knight, who issues him with a strange challenge. What extraordinary thing happens once the challenge has been met?

XVII

Then did the King command that gallant knight to rise,
And swiftly up he gat in fair and courteous wise,
And knelt before his lord, and gripped the axe's haft,
The King, he loosened his hold, and raised his hand aloft,
And blessed him in Christ's Name, and bade him in good part
To be of courage still, hardy of hand and heart.
"Now, Nephew, keep thee well," he quoth, "deal but one blow,
And if thou red'st him well, in very truth I know
The blow that he shall deal thou shalt right well withstand!"
Gawain strode to the knight, the gisarme in his hand,
Right boldly did he bide, no whit abashed, I ween,

And frankly to Gawain he quoth, that knight in green,
"Make we a covenant here, ere yet we further go,
And first I ask, Sir Knight, that I thy name may know,
I bid thee tell me true, that I assured may be –"
"I' faith," quoth that good knight, "Gawain, I wot, is he
Who giveth thee this blow, be it for good or ill,
A twelvemonth hence I'll take another at thy will,
The weapon be thy choice, I'll crave no other still
                              alive!"
                    The other quoth again,
                    "Gawain, so may I thrive,
                    But I shall take full fain,
                    The dint that thou shalt drive!"

XVIII

"By Christ," quoth the Green Knight, "I trow I am full fain
The blow that here I craved to take from thee, Gawain,
And thou hast well rehearsed, in fashion fair, I trow,
The covenant and the boon I prayed the king but now;
Save that thou here, Sir Knight, shalt smoothly swear to me
To seek me out thyself, where e'er it seemeth thee
I may be found on field, and there in turn demand
Such dole as thou shalt deal before this goodly band!"
"Now," quoth the good Gawain, "by Him who fashioned me,
I wot not where to seek, nor where thy home shall be,
I know thee not, Sir Knight, thy court, nor yet thy name,
Teach me thereof the truth, and tell me of that same,
And I will use my wit to win me to that goal,
And here I give thee troth, and swear it on my soul!"
"Nay, in this New Year's tide it needs no more, I ween,"
So to the good Gawain he quoth, that knight in green,

"Save that I tell thee true – when I the blow have ta'en,
Which thou shall smartly smite – and teach thee here amain
Where be my house, my home, and what my name shall be;
Then may'st thou find thy road, and keep thy pledge with me.
But if I waste no speech, thou shalt the better speed,
And in thy land may'st dwell, nor further seek at need
                                    for fight
                    Take thy grim tool to thee
                    Let see how thou can'st smite!"
                    Quoth Gawain, "Willingly,"
                    And stroked his axe so bright.

XIX

The Green Knight on the ground made ready speedily,
He bent his head adown, so that his neck were free,
His long and lovely locks, across the crown they fell,
His bare neck to the nape all men might see right well
Gawain, he gripped his axe, and swung it up on high,
The left foot on the ground he setteth steadily
Upon the neck so bare he let the blade alight,
The sharp edge of the axe the bones asunder smite –
Sheer thro' the flesh it smote, the neck was cleft in two,
The brown steel on the ground it bit, so strong the blow,
The fair head from the neck fell even to the ground,
Spurned by the horse's hoof, e'en as it rolled around,
The red blood spurted forth, and stained the green so bright,
But ne'er for that he failed, nor fell, that stranger knight,
Swiftly he started up, on stiff and steady limb,
And stretching forth his hand, as all men gaped at him,
Grasped at his goodly head, and lift it up again,
Then turned him to his steed, and caught the bridle rein,

Set foot in stirrup-iron, bestrode the saddle fair,
The while he gripped his head e'en by the flowing hair.
He set himself as firm in saddle, so I ween,
As naught had ailed him there, tho' headless he was seen
                              in hall;
                    He turned his steed about,
                    That corpse that bled withal,
                    Full many there had doubt
                    Of how the pledge might fall!

Paul Revere's Ride (excerpt)

Henry Wadsworth Longfellow (1807–1882)

Henry Wadsworth Longfellow was born in Massachusetts, USA. This poem commemorates the actions of Paul Revere in the years leading up to the American Civil War, although it is not entirely historically accurate. The poem opens by directly addressing the reader. Why do you think Longfellow chooses to begin in this way?

Listen, my children, and you shall hear
Of the midnight ride of Paul Revere,
On the eighteenth of April, in Seventy-Five;
Hardly a man is now alive
Who remembers that famous day and year.

He said to his friend, "If the British march
By land or sea from the town to-night,
Hang a lantern aloft in the belfry-arch
Of the North-Church-tower, as a signal-light,–
One if by land, and two, if by sea;
And I on the opposite shore will be,
Ready to ride and spread the alarm
Through every Middlesex village and farm,
For the country-folk to be up and to arm."

Then he said "Good night!" and with muffled oar
Silently rowed to the Charlestown shore,
Just as the moon rose over the bay,
Where swinging wide at her moorings lay
The Somerset, British man-of-war:
A phantom ship, with each mast and spar
Across the moon, like a prison-bar,
And a huge black hulk, that was magnified
By its own reflection in the tide.

Meanwhile, his friend, through alley and street,
Wanders and watches with eager ears,
Till in the silence around him he hears
The muster of men at the barrack door,
The sound of arms, and the tramp of feet,
And the measured tread of the grenadiers,
Marching down to their boats on the shore.

Then he climbed to the tower of the Old North Church,
Up the wooden stairs, with stealthy tread,
To the belfry-chamber overhead,
And startled the pigeons from their perch
On the sombre rafters, that round him made
Masses and moving shapes of shade,–
By the trembling ladder, steep and tall,
To the highest window in the wall,
Where he paused to listen and look down
A moment on the roofs of the town,
And the moonlight flowing over all.
Beneath, in the churchyard, lay the dead,
In their night-encampment on the hill,
Wrapped in silence so deep and still

That he could hear, like a sentinel's tread,
The watchful night-wind, as it went
Creeping along from tent to tent,
And seeming to whisper, "All is well!"
A moment only he feels the spell
Of the place and the hour, and the secret dread
Of the lonely belfry and the dead;
For suddenly all his thoughts are bent
On a shadowy something far away,
Where the river widens to meet the bay, –
A line of black, that bends and floats
On the rising tide, like a bridge of boats.

Meanwhile, impatient to mount and ride,
Booted and spurred, with a heavy stride,
On the opposite shore walked Paul Revere.
Now he patted his horse's side,
Now gazed on the landscape far and near,
Then impetuous stamped the earth,
And turned and tightened his saddle-girth;
But mostly he watched with eager search
The belfry-tower of the Old North Church,
As it rose above the graves on the hill,
Lonely and spectral and sombre and still.
And lo! as he looks, on the belfry's height,
A glimmer, and then a gleam of light!
He springs to the saddle, the bridle he turns,
But lingers and gazes, till full on his sight
A second lamp in the belfry burns!

A hurry of hoofs in a village street,
A shape in the moonlight, a bulk in the dark,
And beneath from the pebbles, in passing, a spark
Struck out by a steed flying fearless and fleet:
That was all! And yet, through the gloom and the light,
The fate of a nation was riding that night;
And the spark struck out by that steed, in his flight,
Kindled the land into flame with its heat.
He has left the village and mounted the steep,
And beneath him, tranquil and broad and deep,
Is the Mystic, meeting the ocean tides;
And under the alders, that skirt its edge,
Now soft on the sand, now load on the ledge,
Is heard the tramp of his steed as he rides.

The Canterbury Tales:
The General Prologue (excerpt)

Geoffrey Chaucer (c.1343–1400)

The *Canterbury Tales* is a collection of over twenty stories written by Geoffrey Chaucer in an old English dialect called "Middle English". The General Prologue, at the start of the Tales, sets the scene for a great pilgrimage that is about to take place. What imagery does Chaucer use to conjure the sense of being ready for a long journey?

The Middle English version is followed by a verse translation in modern English.

Whan that Aprille with his shoures soote
The droghte of Marche hath perced to the roote,
And bathed every veyne in swich licour,
Of which vertu engendred is the flour;
Whan Zephirus eek with his swete breeth
Inspired hath in every holt and heeth
The tendre croppes, and the yonge sonne
Hath in the Ram his halfe cours y-ronne,
And smale fowles maken melodye,
That slepen al the night with open ye,

(So priketh hem nature in hir corages:
Than longen folk to goon on pilgrimages,
And palmers for to seken straunge strondes,
To ferne halwes, couthe in sondry londes;
And specially, from every shires ende
Of Engelond, to Caunterbury they wende,
The holy blisful martir for to seke,
That hem hath holpen, whan that they were seke.

*

When April with his showers sweet with fruit
The drought of March has pierced unto the root
And bathed each vein with liquor that has power
To generate therein and sire the flower;
When Zephyr also has, with his sweet breath,
Quickened again, in every holt and heath,
The tender shoots and buds, and the young sun
Into the Ram one half his course has run,
And many little birds make melody
That sleep through all the night with open eye
(So Nature pricks them on to ramp and rage)—
Then do folk long to go on pilgrimage,
And palmers to go seeking out strange strands,
To distant shrines well known in sundry lands.
And specially from every shire's end
Of England they to Canterbury wend,
The holy blessed martyr there to seek
Who helped them when they lay so ill and weak.

WHAT IT IS
TO BE HUMAN

If

Rudyard Kipling (1865–1936)

Rudyard Kipling was born in India to British parents. He was awarded the Nobel Prize for Literature in 1907. In this famous poem, a father offers advice to his son. What characteristics make up his ideal man? Do you agree, or are there other qualities you would add?

If you can keep your head when all about you
    Are losing theirs and blaming it on you,
If you can trust yourself when all men doubt you,
    But make allowance for their doubting too;
If you can wait and not be tired by waiting,
    Or being lied about, don't deal in lies,
Or being hated, don't give way to hating,
    And yet don't look too good, nor talk too wise:

If you can dream – and not make dreams your master;
    If you can think – and not make thoughts your aim;
If you can meet with Triumph and Disaster
    And treat those two impostors just the same;
If you can bear to hear the truth you've spoken
    Twisted by knaves to make a trap for fools,
Or watch the things you gave your life to, broken,
    And stoop and build 'em up with worn-out tools:

If you can make one heap of all your winnings
    And risk it on one turn of pitch-and-toss,
And lose, and start again at your beginnings
    And never breathe a word about your loss;
If you can force your heart and nerve and sinew
    To serve your turn long after they are gone,
And so hold on when there is nothing in you
    Except the Will which says to them: "Hold on!"

If you can talk with crowds and keep your virtue,
    Or walk with Kings – nor lose the common touch,
If neither foes nor loving friends can hurt you,
    If all men count with you, but none too much;
If you can fill the unforgiving minute
    With sixty seconds' worth of distance run,
Yours is the Earth and everything that's in it,
    And – which is more – you'll be a Man, my son!

My Heart's in the Highlands

Robert Burns (1759–1796)

Robert Burns' poems have become a strong part of Scottish identity. On 25th January every year, his birthday is celebrated – both in Scotland and beyond – with Burns Night dinners, at which his work is traditionally read aloud. Can you spot Burns' use of alliteration and repetition? How does this intensely patriotic poem make you feel?

Farewell to the Highlands, farewell to the North,
The birthplace of Valour, the country of Worth;
Wherever I wander, wherever I rove,
The hills of the Highlands for ever I love.

My heart's in the Highlands, my heart is not here;
My heart's in the Highlands, a-chasing the deer;
Chasing the wild deer, and following the roe,
My heart's in the Highlands, wherever I go.

Farewell to the mountains, high cover'd with snow;
Farewell to the straths and green valleys below;
Farewell to the forests and wild-hanging woods;
Farewell to the torrents and loud-pouring floods.

My heart's in the Highlands, my heart is not here;
My heart's in the Highlands, a-chasing the deer;
Chasing the wild deer, and following the roe –
My heart's in the Highlands wherever I go.

Happy Thought

Robert Louis Stevenson (1850–1894)

This is the shortest poem in the collection: a single rhyming couplet. The title of the poem is simple and positive. Do the ideas in the poem agree or disagree with the title?

> The world is so full of a number of things,
> I'm sure we should be as happy as kings.

No Man Is an Island

John Donne (1572–1631)

John Donne was an English poet and clergyman. He often wrote about abstract themes such as love and belief. In this poem Donne uses the metaphor of an island to explore sense of self. The poem has no obvious rhyme schem

No man is an island,
Entire of itself;
Every man is a piece of the continent,
A part of the main.
If a clod be washed away by the sea,
Europe is the less.
As well as if a promontory were,
As well as if a manor of thy friend's
Or of thine own were,
Any man's death diminishes me,
Because I am involved in mankind,
And therefore never send to know for whom the bell tolls;
It tolls for thee.

The Arrow and the Song

Henry Wadsworth Longfellow (1807–1882)

Henry Wadsworth Longfellow was an American poet, whose first poem was published at the age of 13. What do you think the arrow and song represent in this poem? Compare the first and second stanzas. Do you notice a difference in tone?

I shot an arrow into the air,
It fell to earth, I knew not where;
For, so swiftly it flew, the sight
Could not follow it in its flight.

I breathed a song into the air,
It fell to earth, I knew not where;
For who has sight so keen and strong,
That it can follow the flight of song?

Long, long afterward, in an oak
I found the arrow, still unbroke;
And the song, from beginning to end,
I found again in the heart of a friend.

Jerusalem

William Blake (1757–1827)

Originally written as a poem, "Jerusalem" was set to music by Hubert Parry in 1916. At a time when the First World War was raging, an uplifting patriotic hymn was much needed. What language does Blake use to make England seem glorify or appealing?

And did those feet in ancient time
Walk upon England's mountains green?
And was the holy Lamb of God
On England's pleasant pastures seen?

And did the countenance divine
Shine forth upon our clouded hills?
And was Jerusalem builded here
Among these dark satanic mills?

Bring me my bow of burning gold!
Bring me my arrows of desire!
Bring me my spear! O clouds, unfold!
Bring me my chariot of fire!

I will not cease from mental fight,
Nor shall my sword sleep in my hand,
Till we have built Jerusalem
In England's green and pleasant land

I'm Nobody! Who Are You?

Emily Dickinson (1830–1886)

Emily Dickinson was one of America's best-known female poets. She lived an isolated life in Massachusetts, USA and, despite writing nearly 1800 poems, she published fewer than a dozen in her lifetime. Do you think the persona of this poem is Dickinson herself? Why does the persona like being a "nobody"?

I'm Nobody! Who are you?
Are you – Nobody – too?
Then there's a pair of us!
Don't tell! they'd advertise – you know!

How dreary – to be – Somebody!
How public – like a Frog –
To tell one's name – the livelong June –
To an admiring Bog!

Composed 1554–5

Queen Elizabeth I (1533–1603)

Queen Elizabeth I was the daughter of King Henry VIII and the last Tudor monarch of England. As well as being a generous patron of the arts – and therefore the subject of many poets' work – she also wrote her own poetry. These brief but poignant lines were found scratched on to a window at Woodstock Castle, where Elizabeth was imprisoned during the Protestant uprising. What is the effect of the monarch referring to herself in the third person?

Much suspected by me,
Nothing proved can be,
Quoth Elizabeth prisoner.

Swing Low, Sweet Chariot

Wallis Willis (c. 1820–1880)

"Swing Low Sweet Chariot" was written by Wallis Willis, who was the black slave of a Choctaw Indian (a Native American Tribe). The form is known as a "spiritual": a type of song created by slaves. Faith and hope are key themes in spirituals. What language does Willis use to evoke them here?

Swing low, sweet chariot
Coming for to carry me home,
Swing low, sweet chariot,
Coming for to carry me home.

I looked over Jordan, and what did I see
Coming for to carry me home?
A band of angels coming after me,
Coming for to carry me home.

Chorus

Sometimes I'm up, and sometimes I'm down,
(Coming for to carry me home)
But still my soul feels heavenly bound.
(Coming for to carry me home)

The brightest day that I can say,
(Coming for to carry me home)
When Jesus washed my sins away.
(Coming for to carry me home)

Chorus

If you get there before I do,
(Coming for to carry me home)
Tell all my friends I'm coming there too.
(Coming for to carry me home)

A Poison Tree

William Blake (1757–1827)

In this poem from William Blake's collection *Songs of Experience*, he explores the darker side of the human character via the use of metaphor. What happens when the speaker shares his angry feelings? And what happens when he keeps his feelings bottled up inside?

I was angry with my friend:
I told my wrath, my wrath did end.
I was angry with my foe:
I told it not, my wrath did grow.

And I watered it in fears,
Night & morning with my tears;
And I sunnéd it with smiles,
And with soft deceitful wiles.

And it grew both day and night,
Till it bore an apple bright;
And my foe beheld it shine,
And he knew that it was mine,

And into my garden stole,
When the night had veil'd the pole;
In the morning glad I see
My foe outstretched beneath the tree.

Lift Every Voice and Sing

James Weldon Johnson (1871–1938)

James Weldon Johnson wrote this poem in 1900 for the annual celebration of President Lincoln's birth. It was quickly taken up by the National Association for the Advancement of Colored People as the unofficial "Black American National Anthem". Anthems have to be uplifting and rousing. What emotive language does Johnson use?

Lift every voice and sing
Till earth and heaven ring,
Ring with the harmonies of Liberty;
Let our rejoicing rise,
High as the listening skies,
Let it resound loud as the rolling sea
Sing a song full of faith that the dark past has taught us,
Sing a song full of the hope that the present has brought us;
Facing the rising sun of our
New day begun,
Let us march on till victory is won.

Stony the road we trod,
Bitter the chast'ning rod,
Felt in the day when hope unborn had died;
Yet with a steady beat,
Have not our weary feet,
Come to the place for which our fathers sighed?

We have come over a way that with tears has been watered,
We have come, treading our path through the blood of the
    slaughtered,
Out from the gloomy past,
Till now we stand at last
Where the white gleam of our star is cast.

God of our weary years,
God of our silent tears,
Thou who hast brought us thus far on the way;
Thou who hast by Thy might,
Led us into the light,
Keep us forever in the path, we pray.
Lest our feet stray from the places, our God, where we met
    thee,
Lest our hearts, drunk with the wine of the world, we forget
    thee,
Shadowed beneath Thy hand,
May we forever stand,
True to our God,
True to our native land.

LOVE

Sonnet 18

William Shakespeare (1564–1616)

William Shakespeare wrote 154 sonnets during his lifetime, of which "Sonnet 18" is among the best known. The sonnet form is associated with love poetry and is always made up of 14 lines. In this example, the rhyme pattern is regular until the final couplet. What effect does this change create?

Shall I compare thee to a summer's day?
Thou art more lovely and more temperate:
Rough winds do shake the darling buds of May,
And summer's lease hath all too short a date;
Sometime too hot the eye of heaven shines,
And often is his gold complexion dimmed;
And every fair from fair sometimes declines,
By chance or nature's changing course untrimmed;
But thy eternal summer shall not fade,
Nor lose possession of that fair thou ow'st;
Nor shall death brag thou wand'rest in his shade,
When in eternal lines to Time thou grow'st:
    So long as men can breathe, or eyes can see,
    So long lives this, and this gives life to thee.

When You Are Old

W. B. Yeats (1865–1939)

W. B. Yeats was an Irish poet involved in the Irish Literary Revival. This nostalgic poem explores love in various forms, particularly unrequited love. What techniques does Yeats use to give poignancy to the situation of both the elderly woman and her erstwhile lover?

When you are old and grey and full of sleep,
And nodding by the fire, take down this book,
And slowly read, and dream of the soft look
Your eyes had once, and of their shadows deep;

How many loved your moments of glad grace,
And loved your beauty with love false or true,
But one man loved the pilgrim soul in you,
And loved the sorrows of your changing face;

And bending down beside the glowing bars,
Murmur, a little sadly, how Love fled
And paced upon the mountains overhead
And hid his face amid a crowd of stars.

How Do I Love Thee?

Elizabeth Barrett Browning (1806–1861)

Elizabeth Barrett Browning is an English poet of the Victorian era. This famous love poem is another example of a sonnet. Sonnets can have different rhyme schemes depending on their form. What is the rhyme scheme that Barrett Browning uses here?

How do I love thee? Let me count the ways.
I love thee to the depth and breadth and height
My soul can reach, when feeling out of sight
For the ends of being and ideal grace.
I love thee to the level of every day's
Most quiet need, by sun and candle-light.
I love thee freely, as men strive for right.
I love thee purely, as they turn from praise.
I love thee with the passion put to use
In my old griefs, and with my childhood's faith.
I love thee with a love I seemed to lose
With my lost saints. I love thee with the breath,
Smiles, tears, of all my life; and, if God choose,
I shall but love thee better after death.

A Red, Red Rose

Robert Burns (1759–1796)

This poem is written in Scottish dialect: the spelling of the words reflect Scottish pronunciation. Which words appear differently from the spelling you are used to? The poem is full of symbolic imagery. What do you think the simile "a red, red rose" suggests about love?

O my luve's like a red, red rose,
      That's newly sprung in June;
O my luve's like the melodie
      That's sweetly played in tune.

As fair art thou, my bonnie lass,
      So deep in luve am I;
And I will luve thee still, my dear,
      Till a' the seas gang dry.

Till a' the seas gang dry, my dear,
      And the rocks melt wi' the sun:
O I will luve thee still, my dear,
      While the sands o' life shall run.

And fare thee weel, my only luve,
      And fare thee weel a while!
And I will come again, my luve,
      Though it were ten thousand mile.

Love Not Me for Comely Grace

John Wilbye (1574–1638)

John Wilbye is a poet famous for composing madrigals, non-religious songs performed by several voices. In this poem the speaker suggests that looks are not the most important reason to love someone. What is his explanation? Do you like his idea of how love should be?

Love not me for comely grace,
For my pleasing eye or face;
Nor for any outward part,
No, nor for my constant heart:
    For those may fail or turn to ill,
    So thou and I shall sever.
Keep therefore a true woman's eye,
And love me still, but know not why;
    So hast thou the same reason still
    To doat upon me ever.

Answer to a Child's Question

Samuel Taylor Coleridge (1772–1834)

Samuel Taylor Coleridge was a founding member of the Romantic Movement. This poem gives a voice to the birds so that they can tell us about their love. How does this poem make you feel? Can you identify the words and phrases that give you this feeling?

Do you ask what the birds say? The sparrow, the dove,
The linnet and thrush say, "I love and I love!"
In the winter they're silent, the wind is so strong;
What it says, I don't know, but it sings a loud song.
But green leaves, and blossoms, and sunny warm weather,
And singing, and loving, all come back together!
But the lark is so brimful of gladness and love,
(The green fields below him, the blue sky above),
That he sings, and he sings, and for ever sings he:
"I love my love, and my love loves me!"

Scarborough Fair

Traditional

"Scarborough Fair" is a traditional English ballad that originates from a Scottish ballad called "The Elfin Knight", dating back to around 1670. A man and a woman each give instructions for a series of tasks that their love must perform. What tasks do they set? Are they realistic – and if not, why is this?

(both)
Are you going to Scarborough Fair?
Parsley, sage, rosemary and thyme,
Remember me to one who lives there,
For she once was a true love of mine.

(man)
Tell her to make me a cambric shirt,
Parsley, sage, rosemary and thyme,
Without any seam nor needlework,
And then she'll be a true love of mine.

Tell her to wash it in yonder dry well,
Parsley, sage, rosemary and thyme,
Which never sprung water nor rain ever fell,
And then she'll be a true love of mine.

Tell her to dry it on yonder thorn,
Parsley, sage, rosemary and thyme,
Which never bore blossom since Adam was born,
And then she'll be a true love of mine.

Ask her to do me this courtesy,
Parsley, sage, rosemary and thyme,
And ask for a like favour from me,
And then she'll be a true love of mine.

(both)
Have you been to Scarborough Fair?
Parsley, sage, rosemary and thyme,
Remember me from one who lives there,
For he once was a true love of mine.

(woman)
Ask him to find me an acre of land,
Parsley, sage, rosemary and thyme,
Between the salt water and the sea-sand,
For then he'll be a true love of mine.

Ask him to plough it with a lamb's horn,
Parsley, sage, rosemary and thyme,
And sow it all over with one peppercorn,
For then he'll be a true love of mine.

Ask him to reap it with a sickle of leather,
Parsley, sage, rosemary and thyme,
And gather it up with a rope made of heather,
For then he'll be a true love of mine.

When he has done and finished his work,
Parsley, sage, rosemary and thyme,
Ask him to come for his cambric shirt,
For then he'll be a true love of mine.

(both)
If you say that you can't, then I shall reply,
Parsley, sage, rosemary and thyme,
Oh, Let me know that at least you will try,
Or you'll never be a true love of mine.

Love imposes impossible tasks,
Parsley, sage, rosemary and thyme,
But none more than any heart would ask,
I must know you're a true love of mine.

The Raven (excerpt)

Edgar Allen Poe (1809–1849)

American writer Edgar Allen Poe's "The Raven" is a narrative poem:
it tells a story, in this case the tale of a young man who has lost his
true love, Leonore, and is driven mad by an unexpected visitor. Poe
considered using a parrot instead of a raven in the poem. Would this
have been as effective?

> Once upon a midnight dreary, while I pondered, weak and
>> weary,
> Over many a quaint and curious volume of forgotten lore—
> While I nodded, nearly napping, suddenly there came a tapping,
> As of some one gently rapping, rapping at my chamber door.
> "'Tis some visitor," I muttered, "tapping at my chamber door—
>> Only this, and nothing more."

> Ah, distinctly I remember it was in the bleak December,
> And each separate dying ember wrought its ghost upon the
>> floor.
> Eagerly I wished the morrow;— vainly I had sought to borrow
> From my books surcease of sorrow- sorrow for the lost
>> Lenore—
> For the rare and radiant maiden whom the angels name
>> Lenore—
>> Nameless *here* for evermore.

And the silken, sad, uncertain rustling of each purple curtain
Thrilled me—filled me with fantastic terrors never felt
      before;
So that now, to still the beating of my heart, I stood
      repeating,
"'Tis some visitor entreating entrance at my chamber door—
Some late visitor entreating entrance at my chamber door;—
              This it is, and nothing more."

Presently my soul grew stronger; hesitating then no longer,
"Sir," said I, "or Madam, truly your forgiveness I implore;
But the fact is I was napping, and so gently you came rapping,
And so faintly you came tapping, tapping at my chamber
      door,
That I scarce was sure I heard you"—here I opened wide the
      door;—
              Darkness there, and nothing more.

Deep into that darkness peering, long I stood there
      wondering, fearing,
Doubting, dreaming dreams no mortals ever dared to dream
      before;
But the silence was unbroken, and the stillness gave no token,
And the only word there spoken was the whispered word,
      "Lenore!"
This I whispered, and an echo murmured back the word,
      "Lenore!"
              Merely this, and nothing more.

Back into the chamber turning, all my soul within me
    burning,
Soon again I heard a tapping somewhat louder than before.
"Surely," said I, "surely that is something at my window
    lattice:
Let me see, then, what thereat is, and this mystery explore—
Let my heart be still a moment and this mystery explore;—
                'Tis the wind and nothing more."

Open here I flung the shutter, when, with many a flirt and
    flutter,
In there stepped a stately Raven of the saintly days of yore;
Not the least obeisance made he; not a minute stopped or
    stayed he;
But, with mien of lord or lady, perched above my chamber
    door—
Perched upon a bust of Pallas just above my chamber door—
                Perched, and sat, and nothing more.

Then this ebony bird beguiling my sad fancy into smiling,
By the grave and stern decorum of the countenance it wore.
"Though thy crest be shorn and shaven, thou," I said, "art sure
    no craven,
Ghastly grim and ancient Raven wandering from the Nightly
    shore—
Tell me what thy lordly name is on the Night's Plutonian
    shore!"
                Quoth the Raven, "Nevermore."

Much I marvelled this ungainly fowl to hear discourse so
    plainly,
Though its answer little meaning—little relevancy bore;
For we cannot help agreeing that no living human being
Ever yet was blest with seeing bird above his chamber door—
Bird or beast upon the sculptured bust above his chamber
    door,
                    With such name as "Nevermore."

But the Raven, sitting lonely on the placid bust, spoke only
That one word, as if his soul in that one word he did outpour.
Nothing further then he uttered—not a feather then he
    fluttered—
Till I scarcely more than muttered, "other friends have flown
    before—
On the morrow he will leave me, as my hopes have flown
    before."
                    Then the bird said, "Nevermore."

WAR AND DEATH

The Charge of the Light Brigade

Alfred, Lord Tennyson (1809–1892)

"The Charge of the Light Brigade" has as its subject the Battle of the Balaclava during the Crimean War. What techniques does Tennyson use to evoke the experience of war? Look in particular at the use of repetition and the poem's irregular rhyme scheme. What do they conjure?

Half a league, half a league,
    Half a league onward,
All in the valley of Death
    Rode the six hundred:
"Forward, the Light Brigade!
Charge for the guns!" he said:
Into the valley of Death
    Rode the six hundred.

"Forward, the Light Brigade!"
Was there a man dismay'd?
Not tho' the soldier knew
    Someone had blunder'd:
Theirs not to make reply,
Theirs not to reason why,
Theirs but to do & die,
Into the valley of Death
    Rode the six hundred.

Cannon to right of them,
Cannon to left of them,
Cannon in front of them
    Volley'd & thunder'd;
Storm'd at with shot and shell,
Boldly they rode and well,
Into the jaws of Death,
Into the mouth of Hell
    Rode the six hundred.

Flash'd all their sabres bare,
Flash'd as they turn'd in air
Sabring the gunners there,
Charging an army, while
    All the world wonder'd:
Plunged in the battery-smoke
Right thro' the line they broke;
Cossack & Russian
Reel'd from the sabre-stroke,
    Shatter'd & sunder'd.
Then they rode back, but not
    Not the six hundred.

Cannon to right of them,
Cannon to left of them,
Cannon behind them
    Volley'd and thunder'd;
Storm'd at with shot and shell,
While horse & hero fell,

They that had fought so well
Came thro' the jaws of Death,
Back from the mouth of Hell,
All that was left of them,
     Left of six hundred.

When can their glory fade?
O the wild charge they made!
     All the world wonder'd.
Honour the charge they made!
Honour the Light Brigade,
     Noble six hundred!

Dulce et Decorum Est

Wilfred Owen (1893–1918)

Wilfred Owen is famous for writing about his experiences as a soldier during the First World War. He was interested in the "pity of war": creating poems that cause the reader to empathize with the soldiers' suffering. What similes does Owen use to describe the horror of war? The final Latin phrase at the end of the poem translates as "It is sweet and right to die for your country". Do you think Owen believes this?

Bent double, like old beggars under sacks,
Knock-kneed, coughing like hags, we cursed through sludge,
Till on the haunting flares we turned our backs
And towards our distant rest began to trudge.
Men marched asleep. Many had lost their boots,
But limped on, blood-shod. All went lame, all blind;
Drunk with fatigue; deaf even to the hoots
Of tired, outstripped Five-Nines that dropped behind.

Gas! GAS! Quick, boys! – An ecstasy of fumbling,
Fitting the clumsy helmets just in time;
But someone still was yelling out and stumbling,
And floundering like a man in fire or lime…
Dim through the misty panes and thick green light,
As under a green sea, I saw him drowning.

In all my dreams, before my helpless sight,
He plunges at me, guttering, choking, drowning.

If in some smothering dreams, you too could pace
Behind the wagon that we flung him in,
And watch the white eyes writhing in his face,
His hanging face, like a devil's sick of sin;
If you could hear, at every jolt, the blood
Come gargling from the froth-corrupted lungs,
Obscene as cancer, bitter as the cud
Of vile, incurable sores on innocent tongues,—
My friend, you would not tell with such high zest
To children ardent for some desperate glory,
The old Lie: Dulce et decorum est
Pro patria mori.

Here Dead We Lie

A. E. Housman (1859–1936)

This famous poem, written in 1914, adopts the voice of a fallen soldier. The first stanza suggests that it is better to fight and die, than to be a coward. The second stanza complicates this choice. How do the final lines make you feel and can you explain why?

Here dead we lie
Because we did not choose
To live and shame the land
From which we sprung.

Life, to be sure,
Is nothing much to lose,
But young men think it is,
And we were young.

In Flanders Fields

John McCrae (1872–1918)

John McCrae was a military doctor during the First World War. This poem was inspired by his experience conducting a burial at the front, and gave rise to the tradition of using of poppies to commemorate fallen soldiers. As in A. E. Housman's poem, the voice is that of the dead soldiers. What similarities and differences can you see between the two poems?

In Flanders fields the poppies blow
Between the crosses, row on row,
That mark our place; and in the sky
The larks, still bravely singing, fly
Scarce heard amid the guns below.

We are the Dead. Short days ago
We lived, felt dawn, saw sunset glow,
Loved and were loved, and now we lie
In Flanders fields.

Take up our quarrel with the foe:
To you from failing hands we throw
The torch; be yours to hold it high.
If ye break faith with us who die
We shall not sleep, though poppies grow
In Flanders fields.

Invictus

W. E. Henley (1849–1903)

William Ernest Henley was an English poet and critic. Strength and determination are key themes in Henley's poem, written in 1875: the title "Invictus" is a Latin word meaning "unconquered". What does the speaker in this poem overcome? The poem is set at night-time. What else does Henley use images of darkness to represent?

Out of the night that covers me,
    Black as the pit from pole to pole,
I thank whatever gods may be
    For my unconquerable soul.

In the fell clutch of circumstance
    I have not winced nor cried aloud.
Under the bludgeonings of chance
    My head is bloody, but unbow'd.

Beyond this place of wrath and tears
    Looms but the Horror of the shade,
And yet the menace of the years
    Finds, and shall find, me unafraid.

It matters not how strait the gate,
    How charged with punishments the scroll,
I am the master of my fate;
    I am the captain of my soul.

The Soldier

Rupert Brooke (1887–1915)

In contrast to Wilfred Owen's interest in the "pity of war", Rupert Brooke writes idealistically about the First World War. How does this poem, written while Brooke was on military leave in 1914, convey a sense of patriotism?

If I should die, think only this of me:
    That there's some corner of a foreign field
That is for ever England. There shall be
    In that rich earth a richer dust concealed;
A dust whom England bore, shaped, made aware,
    Gave, once, her flowers to love, her ways to roam,
A body of England's, breathing English air,
    Washed by the rivers, blest by suns of home.

And think, this heart, all evil shed away,
    A pulse in the eternal mind, no less
        Gives somewhere back the thoughts by England given;
Her sights and sounds; dreams happy as her day;
    And laughter, learnt of friends; and gentleness,
        In hearts at peace, under an English heaven.

The Mother

Padraig Pearse (1879–1916)

Padraig Pearse was an Irish writer, widely recognized as the main voice of the Easter Rising of 1916, an armed uprising in which Irish republicans sought to overthrow British rule. While Rupert Brooke writes about conflict in a foreign land, Pearse's poem focuses on suffering at home. The poem is written in "free verse" – it has no rhyme scheme. What effect does this have on how you read the poem?

I do not grudge them; Lord, I do not grudge
My two strong sons that I have seen go out
To break their strength and die, they and a few,
In bloody protest for a glorious thing.
They shall be spoken of among their people,
The generations shall remember them,
And call them blessed;
But I will speak their names to my own heart
In the long nights;
The little names that were familiar once
Round my dead hearth.
Lord, thou art hard on mothers:
We suffer in their coming and their going;
And tho' I grudge them not, I weary, weary
Of the long sorrow – And yet I have my joy:
My sons were faithful, and they fought.

Futility

Wilfred Owen (1893–1918)

Wilfred Owen was sent to fight in the First World War aged just eighteen. By personifying the sun, Owen suggests it is being used as a metaphor. What do you it represents? The poem opens with an imperative: "move". How does this contrast with the poem's title and the message of the final lines?

Move him into the sun—
Gently its touch awoke him once,
At home, whispering of fields half-sown.
Always it woke him, even in France,
Until this morning and this snow.
If anything might rouse him now
The kind old sun will know.

Think how it wakes the seeds,—
Woke once the clays of a cold star.
Are limbs, so dear-achieved, are sides
Full-nerved, still warm, too hard to stir?
Was it for this the clay grew tall?
—O what made fatuous sunbeams toil
To break earth's sleep at all?

FAIRYTALE
AND FANTASY

The Rime of the Ancient Mariner (excerpt)

Samuel Taylor Coleridge (1772–1834)

This famous ballad tells of a mariner's adventures on the high seas. When a ship strays off course in Antarctic waters, an albatross appears and guides it to safety. Despite this, the mariner shoots it and brings bad luck to the ship – including, in this extract, running out of drinking water. What language does Coleridge use to show that the ship has been cursed? How does the crew punish the mariner?

Water, water, every where,
And all the boards did shrink;
Water, water, every where,
Nor any drop to drink.

The very deep did rot: O Christ!
That ever this should be!
Yea, slimy things did crawl with legs
Upon the slimy sea.

About, about, in reel and rout
The death-fires danced at night;
The water, like a witch's oils,
Burnt green, and blue and white.

And some in dreams assuréd were
Of the Spirit that plagued us so;
Nine fathom deep he had followed us
From the land of mist and snow.

And every tongue, through utter drought,
Was withered at the root;
We could not speak, no more than if
We had been choked with soot.

Ah! well a-day! what evil looks
Had I from old and young!
Instead of the cross, the Albatross
About my neck was hung.

The Kraken

Alfred, Lord Tennyson (1809–1892)

The Kraken is a legendary sea monster that resembles a giant octopus. Tennyson provides little description of the Kraken itself, focusing instead on the creatures that surround it. Why do you think he chooses to do this, and do you find it effective?

Below the thunders of the upper deep;
Far, far beneath in the abysmal sea,
His ancient, dreamless, uninvaded sleep
The Kraken sleepeth: faintest sunlights flee
About his shadowy sides: above him swell
Huge sponges of millennial growth and height;
And far away into the sickly light,
From many a wondrous grot and secret cell
Unnumbered and enormous polypi
Winnow with giant arms the slumbering green.
There hath he lain for ages and will lie
Battening upon huge sea-worms in his sleep,
Until the latter fire shall heat the deep;
Then once by man and angels to be seen,
In roaring he shall rise and on the surface die.

Over Hill, Over Dale (excerpt from *A Midsummer Night's Dream*)

William Shakespeare (1564–1616)

This speech from *A Midsummer Night's Dream* is spoken by one of the fairies who serves Titania, the Fairy Queen, and describes some of the tasks she must perform. How does the language and rhythm conjure the feeling of a fairy world?

Over hill, over dale,
Thorough bush, thorough brier,
Over park, over pale,
Thorough flood, thorough fire;
I do wander everywhere,
Swifter than the moon's sphere;
And I serve the Fairy Queen,
To dew her orbs upon the green.
The cowslips tall her pensioners be;
In their gold coats spots you see;
Those be rubies, fairy favours;
In those freckles live their savours;
I must go seek some dewdrops here,
And hang a pearl in every cowslip's ear.

Beowulf – The Fight With Grendel (excerpt)

Anonymous, translated by Lesslie Hall (1856–1938)

Beowulf is an Old English epic poem that, in its entirety, is 3182 lines long. It tells the story of a warrior, Beowulf, who is sent by the king to fight Grendel, a monster who has been terrorizing the community. In this excerpt, we meet Grendel as he sneaks into town to attack the Great Hall.

'Neath the cloudy cliffs came from the moor then
Grendel going, God's anger bare he.
The monster intended some one of earthmen
In the hall-building grand to entrap and make way with:
He went under welkin where well he knew of
The wine-joyous building, brilliant with plating,
Gold-hall of earthmen. Not the earliest occasion
He the home and manor of Hrothgar had sought:
Ne'er found he in life-days later nor earlier
Hardier hero, hall-thanes more sturdy!
Then came to the building the warrior marching,
Bereft of his joyance. The door quickly opened
On fire-hinges fastened, when his fingers had touched it;
The fell one had flung then—his fury so bitter—
Open the entrance. Early thereafter
The foeman trod the shining hall-pavement,
Strode he angrily; from the eyes of him glimmered
A lustre unlovely likest to fire.

He beheld in the hall the heroes in numbers,
A circle of kinsmen sleeping together,
A throng of thanemen: then his thoughts were exultant,
He minded to sunder from each of the thanemen
The life from his body, horrible demon,
Ere morning came, since fate had allowed him
The prospect of plenty. Providence willed not
To permit him any more of men under heaven
To eat in the night-time. Higelac's kinsman
Great sorrow endured how the dire-mooded creature
In unlooked-for assaults were likely to bear him.
No thought had the monster of deferring the matter,
But on earliest occasion he quickly laid hold of
A soldier asleep, suddenly tore him,
Bit his bone-prison, the blood drank in currents,
Swallowed in mouthfuls: he soon had the dead man's
Feet and hands, too, eaten entirely.

Double, Double, Toil and Trouble
(excerpt from Macbeth)

William Shakespeare (1564–1616)

These verses come from William Shakespeare's play, *Macbeth*. In the drama, three witches convince Macbeth to pursue the Scottish throne. In this excerpt they make a potion to bewitch him. What do you think the refrain "double, double toil and trouble/fire burn and cauldron bubble" means?

Double, Double toil and trouble;
Fire, burn; and cauldron bubble.
Fillet of a fenny snake,
In the caldron boil and bake;
Eye of newt, and toe of frong,
Wool of bat, and tongue of dog,
Adder's fork, and blind-worm's sting,
Lizard's leg, and howlet's wing,
For a charm of powerful trouble,
Like a hell-broth boil and bubble.

Double, double toil and trouble,
Fire, burn; and cauldron, bubble.
Cool it with a baboon's blood:
Then the charm is firm and good.

If We Shadows Have Offended (excerpt from *A Midsummer Night's Dream*)

William Shakespeare (1564–1616)

This is an extract from the epilogue (the final section) of *A Midsummer Night's Dream*. The play has taken place in a forest outside Athens, where mischievous fairies play tricks on four young lovers. Here, Robin addresses the audience, apologizing for the trouble the fairies have caused. What does he suggest might have happened to the audience while the action has been taking place?

If we shadows have offended,
Think but this, and all is mended,
That you have but slumbered here,
While these visions did appear.
And this weak and idle theme,
No more yielding but a dream,
Gentles, do not reprehend:
If you pardon, we will mend:
And, as I am an honest puck,
If we have unearned luck
Now to 'scape the serpent's tongue,
We will make amends ere long,
Else the puck a liar call.
So, good night unto you all.
Give me your hands, if we be friends,
And Robin shall restore amends.

Fairy Song

Louisa May Alcott (1832–1888)

Louisa May Alcott is most famous as the author of *Little Women*, but was also a successful poet. Compare Alcott's depiction of fairies and their world with Shakespeare's in "Over Hill, Over Dale". What similarities and differences do you notice?

The moonlight fades from flower and tree,
    And the stars dim one by one;
The tale is told, the song is sung,
    And the Fairy feast is done.
The night-wind rocks the sleeping flowers,
    And sings to them, soft and low.
The early birds erelong will wake:
    'Tis time for the Elves to go.

O'er the sleeping earth we silently pass,
    Unseen by mortal eye,
And send sweet dreams, as we lightly float
    Through the quiet moonlit sky;
For the stars' soft eyes alone may see,
    And the flowers alone may know,
The feasts we hold, the tales we tell:
    So 'tis time for the Elves to go.

From bird, and blossom, and bee,
    We learn the lessons they teach;
And seek, by kindly deeds, to win
    A loving friend in each.
And though unseen on earth we dwell,
    Sweet voices whisper low,
And gentle hearts most joyously greet
    The Elves where'er they go.

When next we meet in the Fairy dell,
    May the silver moon's soft light
Shine then on faces gay as now,
    And Elfin hearts as light.
Now spread each wing, for the eastern sky
    With sunlight soon will glow.
The morning star shall light us home:
    Farewell! for the Elves must go.

NONSENSE POETRY

The Owl and the Pussycat

Edward Lear (1812–1888)

Edward Lear was an artist, musician, author and poet, best known for his "nonsense poetry". Nonsense poetry uses unusual words and surprising juxtapositions to tell a tale that is funny or unexpected. What strange things happen in this poem?

The Owl and the Pussycat went to sea
    In a beautiful pea-green boat,
They took some honey, and plenty of money,
    Wrapped up in a five-pound note.
The Owl looked up to the stars above,
    And sang to a small guitar,
"O lovely Pussy! O Pussy, my love,
    What a beautiful Pussy you are, you are, you are,
    What a beautiful Pussy you are."

Pussy said to the Owl, "You elegant fowl,
    How charmingly sweet you sing!
O let us be married, too long we have tarried;
    But what shall we do for a ring?"
They sailed away, for a year and a day,
    To the land where the Bong-tree grows,
And there in a wood a Piggy-wig stood
    With a ring at the end of his nose, his nose, his nose,
    With a ring at the end of his nose.

"Dear Pig, are you willing to sell for one shilling
Your ring?" Said the Piggy, "I will"
So they took it away, and were married next day
    By the Turkey who lives on the hill.
They dined on mince, and slices of quince,
    Which they ate with a runcible spoon.
And hand in hand, on the edge of the sand.
    They danced by the light of the moon, the moon, the
        moon,
    They danced by the light of the moon.

The Quangle Wangle's Hat

Edward Lear (1812–1888)

This nonsense poem was first published in 1877 in Edward Lear's book *Laughable Lyrics*. Although many of the words are unfamiliar, but the poem's themes are universal. What do you think its key message is?

On the top of the Crumpetty Tree
    The Quangle Wangle sat,
But his face you could not see,
    On account of his Beaver Hat.
For his Hat was a hundred and two feet wide,
With ribbons and bibbons on every side,
And bells, and buttons, and loops, and lace,
So that nobody ever could see the face
      Of the Quangle Wangle Quee.

The Quangle Wangle said
    To himself on the Crumpetty Tree,
"Jam; and jelly; and bread;
    Are the best food for me!
But the longer I live on this Crumpetty Tree
The plainer than ever it seems to me
That very few people come this way
And that life on the whole is far from gay!"
      Said the Quangle Wangle Quee.

But there came to the Crumpetty Tree,
	Mr and Mrs Canary;
And they said, "Did you ever see
	Any spot so charmingly airy?
May we build a nest on your lovely Hat?
Mr Quangle Wangle, grant us that!
O please let us come and build a nest
Of whatever material suits you best,
		Mr Quangle Wangle Quee!"

And besides, to the Crumetty Tree
	Came the Stork, the Duck, and the Owl;
The Snail, and the Bumble-Bee,
	The Frog, and the Fimble Fowl
(The Fimble Fowl, with a Corkscrew leg);
And all of them said, "We humbly beg,
We may build our homes on your lovely Hat,
Mr Quangle Wangle, grant us that!
		Mr Quangle Wangle Quee!"

And the Golden Grouse came there,
	And the Pobble who has no toes,
And the small Olympian bear,
	And the Dong with a luminous nose.
And the Blue Babboon, who played the flute,
And the Orient Calf from the Land of Tute,
And the Attery Squash, and the Bisky Bat,
All came and built on the lovely Hat
		Of the Quangle Wangle Quee.

And the Quangle Wangle said
    To himself on the Crumpetty Tree,
"When all these creatures move
    What a wonderful noise there'll be!"
And at night by the light of the Mulberry moon
They danced to the flute of the Blue Baboon,
On the broad green leaves of the Crumpetty Tree,
And all were as happy as happy could be,
      With the Quangle Wangle Quee.

A Frog Went A-Courtin'

Anonymous

"A Frog Went A-Courtin'" is a folk song which dates back as far as 1548. Many versions have evolved over the years but this one is the best known. What do you think it is about the rhythm and rhyme of this poem which lends it to being sung?

A frog went a-courtin' and he did ride, M-hm, M-hm.
A frog went a-courtin' and he did ride,
Sword and pistol by his side, M-hm, M-hm.

He rode up to Miss Mousie's door, M-hm, M-hm,
He rode up to Miss Mousie's door,
Where he'd often been before, M-hm, M-hm.

He said, "Miss Mouse, are you within?' M-hm, M-hm,
He said, "Miss Mouse, are you within?"
"Yes, kind sir, I sit and spin". M-hm, M-hm.

He took Miss Mouse upon his knee, M-hm, M-hm,
He took Miss Mouse upon his knee and
Said "Miss Mouse, will you marry me?" M-hm, M-hm.

"Without my Uncle Rat's consent, M-hm, M-hm,
Without my Uncle Rat's consent
I wouldn't marry the President". M-hm, M-hm.

Uncle Rat laughed and shook his fat sides, M-hm, M-hm,
Uncle Rat laughed and shook his fat sides,
To think his niece would be a bride, M-hm, M-hm.

Then Uncle Rat rode off to town, M-hm, M-hm,
Then Uncle Rat rode off to town
To buy his niece a wedding gown, M-hm, M-hm.

"Oh, where will the wedding supper be?" M-hm, M-hm,
"Oh where will the wedding supper be?"
"Way down yonder in the hollow tree". M-hm, M-hm.

The first to come was the little white moth, M-hm, M-hm,
The first to come was the little white moth;
She spread out the tablecloth, M-hm, M-hm.
The next to come was the bumblebee, M-hm, M-hm,
The next to come was the bumblebee who
Played the fiddle upon his knee, M-hm, M-hm.

The next to come was a little flea, M-hm, M-hm,
The next to come was a little flea who
Danced a jig with the bumblebee, M-hm, M-hm.
The next to come was Missus Cow, M-hm, M-hm,
The next to come was Missus Cow who
Tried to dance but didn't know how, M-hm, M-hm.

Now Mister Frog was dressed in green, M-hm, M-hm,
Now Mister Frog was dressed in green and
Sweet Miss Mouse looked like a queen, M-hm, M-hm.
In slowly walked the Parson Rook, M-hm, M-hm,
In slowly walked the Parson Rook;
Under his arm he carried a book, M-hm, M-hm.

They all gathered round the lucky pair, M-hm, M-hm,
They all gathered round the lucky pair,
Singing, dancing everywhere, M-hm, M-hm.
Then Frog and Mouse went off to France, M-hm, M-hm,
Then Frog and Mouse went off to France and
That's the end of my romance, M-hm, M-hm.

The Crocodile (excerpt from *Alice's Adventures in Wonderland*)

Lewis Carroll (1832–1898)

Lewis Carroll was a Victorian writer known for his humorous, and often surreal, writing style. This poem is a parody of another poem, "Against Idleness and Mischief", written by Isaac Watts (1715). The original poem is about the virtue of hard work and good behaviour. How does Lewis Carroll turn these themes on their head?

How doth the little crocodile
    Improve his shining tail,
And pour the waters of the Nile
    On every golden scale!

How cheerfully he seems to grin,
    How neatly spreads his claws,
And welcomes little fishes in,
    With gently smiling jaws!

The Walrus and the Carpenter
(excerpt from *Through the Looking-Glass*)

Lewis Carroll (1832–1898)

"The Walrus and the Carpenter" comes from Carroll's book *Through the Looking-Glass*. Can you notice any themes that it has in common with "The Crocodile"? Do you think the poem attempts to offer a moral message – or the opposite?

The sun was shining on the sea,
    Shining with all his might:
He did his very best to make
    The billows smooth and bright—
And this was odd, because it was
    The middle of the night.

The moon was shining sulkily,
    Because she thought the sun
Had got no business to be there
    After the day was done—
"It's very rude of him," she said,
    "To come and spoil the fun!"

The sea was wet as wet could be,
    The sands were dry as dry.
You could not see a cloud, because
    No cloud was in the sky:
No birds were flying over head—
    There were no birds to fly.

The Walrus and the Carpenter
    Were walking close at hand;
They wept like anything to see
    Such quantities of sand:
"If this were only cleared away,"
    They said, "it would be grand!"

"If seven maids with seven mops
    Swept it for half a year,
Do you suppose," the Walrus said,
    "That they could get it clear?"
"I doubt it," said the Carpenter,
    And shed a bitter tear.

"O Oysters, come and walk with us!"
    The Walrus did beseech.
"A pleasant walk, a pleasant talk,
    Along the briny beach:
We cannot do with more than four,
    To give a hand to each."

The eldest Oyster looked at him.
　　But never a word he said:
The eldest Oyster winked his eye,
　　And shook his heavy head—
Meaning to say he did not choose
　　To leave the oyster-bed.

But four young oysters hurried up,
　　All eager for the treat:
Their coats were brushed, their faces washed,
　　Their shoes were clean and neat—
And this was odd, because, you know,
　　They hadn't any feet.

Four other Oysters followed them,
　　And yet another four;
And thick and fast they came at last,
　　And more, and more, and more—
All hopping through the frothy waves,
　　And scrambling to the shore.

The Walrus and the Carpenter
　　Walked on a mile or so,
And then they rested on a rock
　　Conveniently low:
And all the little Oysters stood
　　And waited in a row.

"The time has come," the Walrus said,
    "To talk of many things:
Of shoes—and ships—and sealing-wax—
    Of cabbages—and kings—
And why the sea is boiling hot—
    And whether pigs have wings."

"But wait a bit," the Oysters cried,
    "Before we have our chat;
For some of us are out of breath,
    And all of us are fat!"
"No hurry!" said the Carpenter.
    They thanked him much for that.

"A loaf of bread," the Walrus said,
    "Is what we chiefly need:
Pepper and vinegar besides
    Are very good indeed—
Now if you're ready Oysters dear,
    We can begin to feed."

"But not on us!" the Oysters cried,
    Turning a little blue,
"After such kindness, that would be
    A dismal thing to do!"
"The night is fine," the Walrus said
    "Do you admire the view?

"It was so kind of you to come!
    And you are very nice!"
The Carpenter said nothing but
    "Cut us another slice:
I wish you were not quite so deaf—
    I've had to ask you twice!"

"It seems a shame," the Walrus said,
    "To play them such a trick,
After we've brought them out so far,
    And made them trot so quick!"
The Carpenter said nothing but
    "The butter's spread too thick!"

"I weep for you," the Walrus said.
    "I deeply sympathize."
With sobs and tears he sorted out
    Those of the largest size.
Holding his pocket handkerchief
    Before his streaming eyes.

"O Oysters," said the Carpenter.
    "You've had a pleasant run!
Shall we be trotting home again?"
    But answer came there none—
And that was scarcely odd, because
    They'd eaten every one.

Jabberwocky (excerpt from *Through the Looking-Glass*)

Lewis Carroll (1832–1898)

"Jabberwocky" is one of the most famous nonsense poems ever written. Although much of the language is made up, it still contains a clear narrative. How many made-up words can you find? Inspired by myths and legends, "Jabberwocky" tells the story of a triumph against a terrifying beast. How does it compare to "Beowulf"?

'Twas brillig, and the slithy toves
    Did gyre and gimble in the wabe:
All mimsy were the borogoves,
    And the mome raths outgrabe.

"Beware the Jabberwock, my son!
    The jaws that bite, the claws that catch!
Beware the Jubjub bird, and shun
    The frumious Bandersnatch!"

He took his vorpal sword in hand:
    Long time the manxome foe he sought –
So rested he by the Tumtum tree,
    And stood awhile in thought.

And, as in uffish thought he stood,
  The Jabberwock, with eyes of flame,
Came wiffling through the tulgey wood,
  And burbled as it came!

One, two! One, two! And through and through
  The vorpal blade went snicker-snack!
He left it dead, and with its head
  He went galumphing back.

"And hast thou slain the Jabberwock?
  Come to my arms, my beamish boy!
O frabjous day! Callooh! Callay!"
  He chortled in his joy.

'Twas brillig, and the slithy toves
  Did gyre and gimble in the wabe:
All mimsy were the borogoves,
  And the mome raths outgrabe.

An Alphabet Poem

Edward Lear (1812–1888)

In this entertaining poem, Edward Lear chooses an animal or object to represent each letter of the alphabet, then creates a short narrative to capture some of its qualities. Which narratives do you find particularly effective in evoking the subject?

A
A was once an apple pie,
Pidy
Widy
Tidy
Pidy
Nice insidy
Apple Pie!

B
B was once a little bear,
Beary!
Wary!
Hairy!
Beary!
Taky cary!
Little Bear!

C
C was once a little cake,
Caky
Baky
Maky
Caky
Taky Caky,
Little Cake!

D
D was once a little doll,
Dolly
Molly
Polly
Nolly
Nursy Dolly
Little Doll!

E
E was once a little eel,
Eely,
Weely
Peely
Eely
Twirly, Tweedy
Little Eel!

F
F was once a little fish,
Fishy
Wishy
Squishy

Fishy
In a Dishy
Little Fish!

G
G was once a little goose,
Goosy
Moosy
Boosy
Goosey
Waddly-woosy
Little Goose!

H
H was once a little hen,
Henny
Chenny
Tenny
Henny
Eggsy-any
Little Hen?

I
I was once a bottle of ink,
Inky
Dinky
Thinky
Inky
Black Minky
Bottle of Ink!

J

J was once a jar of jam,

Jammy

Mammy

Clammy

Jammy

Sweety-Swammy

Jar of Jam!

K

K was once a little kite,

Kity

Whity

Flighty

Kity

Out of sighty

Little Kite!

L

L was once a little lark,

Larky!

Marky!

Harky!

Larky!

In the Parky

Little Lark!

M

M was once a little mouse,

Mousey

Bousey

Sousy

Mousy
In the Housy
Little Mouse!

N
N was once a little needle,
Needly
Tweedly
Threedly
Needly
Wisky-wheedly
Little Needle!

O
O was once a little owl,
Owly
Prowly
Howly
Owly
Browny fowly
Little Owl!

P
P was once a little pump,
Pumpy
Slumpy
Flumpy
Pumpy
Dumpy, Thumpy
Little Pump!

Q

Q was once a little quail,

Quaily

Faily

Daily

Quaily

Stumpy-taily

Little Quail!

R

R was once a little rose,

Rosy

Posy

Nosy

Rosy

Bows-y – grows-y

Little Rose!

S

S was once a little shrimp,

Shrimpy

Nimpy

Flimpy

Shrimpy

Jumpy-jimpy

Little Shrimp!

T

T was once a little thrush,

Thrushy!

Hushy!

Bushy!

Thrushy!
Flitty-Flushy
Little Thrush!

U
U was once a little urn,
Urny
Burny
Turny
Urny
Bubbly-burny
Little Urn!

V
V was once a little vine,
Viny
Winy
Twiny
Viny
Twisty-twiny
Little Vine!

W
W was once a whale,
Whaly
Scaly
Shaly
Whaly
Tumbly-taily
Mighty Whale!

X
X was once a great king Xerxes,
Xerxy
Perxy
Turxy
Xerxy
Linxy Lurxy
Great King Xerxes!

Y
Y was once a little yew,
Yewdy
Fewdy
Crudy
Yewdy
Growdy, grewdy,
Little Yew!

Z
Z was once a piece of zinc,
Tinky
Winky
Blinky
Tinky
Tinkly Minky
Piece of Zinc!

The Mock Turtle's Song (excerpt from *Alice's Adventures in Wonderland*)

Lewis Carroll (1832–1898)

Like "The Crocodile", "The Mock Turtle's Song" is a parody of another poem that was widely known by Victorian children, and which appears in the Rhymes and Riddles section of this book. Can you work out which one it is? The setting of the poem is the seashore. What does the repeated "will you, won't you" refrain remind you of?

"Will you walk a little faster?"
Said a whiting to a snail,
"There's a porpoise close behind us,
And he's treading on my tail.
See how eagerly the lobsters
And the turtles all advance!
They are waiting on the shingle –
Will you come and join the dance?
Will you, won't you, will you,
Won't you, will you join the dance?
Will you, won't you, will you,
Won't you, won't you join the dance?

"You can really have no notion
How delightful it will be
When they take us up and throw us,
With the lobsters, out to sea!"
But the snail replied, "Too far, too far!"
And gave a look askance –
Said he thanked the whiting kindly,
But he would not join the dance.
Would not, could not, would not,
Could not, would not join the dance.
Would not, could not, would not,
Could not, could not join the dance.

"What matters it how far we go?"
His scaly friend replied;
"There is another shore, you know,
Upon the other side.
The further off from England
The nearer is to France –
Then turn not pale, beloved snail,
But come and join the dance.
Will you, won't you, will you,
Won't you, will you join the dance?
Will you, won't you, will you,
Won't you, won't you join the dance?

The Duck and the Kangaroo

Edward Lear (1812–1888)

Edward Lear's nonsense poetry often takes two characters as its subject. In this poem he explores the relationship between a Duck and a Kangaroo. How can we tell that the two creatures have very different personalities?

Said the Duck to the Kangaroo,
    "Good gracious! how you hop!
Over the fields and the water too,
    As if you never would stop!
My life is a bore in this nasty pond,
And I long to go out in the world beyond!
    I wish I could hop like you!"
    Said the Duck to the Kangaroo.

"Please give me a ride on your back!"
    Said the Duck to the Kangaroo.
"I would sit quite still, and say nothing but 'Quack',
    The whole of the long day through!
And we'd go to the Dee, and the Jelly Bo Lee,
Over the land, and over the sea;
    Please take me a ride! O do!"
    Said the Duck to the Kangaroo.

Said the Kangaroo to the Duck,

"This requires some little reflection;

Perhaps on the whole it might bring me luck,

And there seems but one objection,

Which is, if you'll let me speak so bold,

Your feet are unpleasantly wet and cold,

And would probably give me the roo-

Matiz!" said the Kangaroo.

Said the Duck, "As I sat on the rocks,

I have thought over that completely,

And I bought four pairs of worsted socks

Which fit my web-feet neatly.

And to keep out the cold I've bought a cloak,

And every day a cigar I'll smoke,

All to follow my own dear true

Love of a Kangaroo!"

Said the Kangaroo, "I'm ready!

All in the moonlight pale;

But to balance me well, dear Duck, sit steady!

And quite at the end of my tail!"

So away they went with a hop and a bound,

And they hopped the whole world three times round;

And who so happy – O who,

As the Duck and the Kangaroo?

Selected Limericks

Edward Lear (1812–1888)

The limerick form was made popular by Edward Lear's poetry collection, *Book of Nonsense* (1846). Limericks always consist of five lines, use a strict rhyme scheme and are often comical. Try saying these examples out loud while clapping or tapping your feet. What do you notice about the rhythm or metre?

There was an Old Man with a beard,
Who said, "It is just as I feared!—
Two Owls and a Hen,
Four Larks and a Wren,
Have all built their nests in my beard!"

There was an Old Lady of Chertsey,
Who made a remarkable curtsey;
She twirled round and round,
Till she sank underground,
Which distressed all the people of Chertsey.

There was an Old Man who said, "How
Shall I flee from this horrible Cow?
I will sit on this stile,
And continue to smile,
Which may soften the heart of that Cow."

There is a Young Lady, whose nose
Continually prospers and grows;
When it grew out of sight,
She exclaimed in a fright,
"Oh! Farewell to the end of my nose!"

There was an Old Man of Dumbree,
Who taught little owls to drink tea;
For he said, "To eat mice,
Is not proper or nice,"
That amiable Man of Dumbree.

RHYMES
AND
RIDDLES

Twinkle, Twinkle

Jane Taylor (?)

This is one of the best known rhymes ... young children. What do you think each ... adjectives are used to describe ...

Twinkle, twinkle, little star,
How I wonder what you are!
Up above the world so high,
Like a diamond in the sky.

When the blazing sun is gone,
When he nothing shines upon,
Then you show your little light,
Twinkle, twinkle, all the night.

Then the traveller in the dark,
Thanks you for your tiny spark,
He could not see which way to go,
If you did not twinkle so.

In the dark blue sky you keep,
And often through my curtains peep,
For you never shut your eye,
Till the sun is in the sky.

Twinkle, Twinkle, Little Star

Jane Taylor (1783–1824)

This is one of the best known children's poems, often sung to very young children. What do you think the star could symbolize? What adjectives are used to describe it?

Twinkle, twinkle, little star,
How I wonder what you are!
Up above the world so high,
Like a diamond in the sky.

When the blazing sun is gone,
When he nothing shines upon,
Then you show your little light,
Twinkle, twinkle, all the night.

Then the traveller in the dark
Thanks you for your tiny spark;
He could not see which way to go,
If you did not twinkle so.

In the dark blue sky you keep,
And often through my curtains peep,
For you never shut your eye
Till the sun is in the sky.

As your bright and tiny spark
Lights the traveller in the dark,
Though I know not what you are,
Twinkle, twinkle, little star.

The Spider and the Fly

Mary Howitt (1799–1888)

Mary Howitt was brought up as a Quaker and many of her works include a moral message. What do you think the moral of this poem is? This poem is a dialogue poem. Why do you think Howitt chose to write in this form?

"Will you walk into my parlour?" said the Spider to the Fly,
"'Tis the prettiest little parlour that ever you did spy;
The way into my parlour is up a winding stair,
And I've a many curious things to show when you are there."
"Oh no, no," said the little Fly, "to ask me is in vain,
For who goes up your winding stair can ne'er come down
       again."

"I'm sure you must be weary, dear, with soaring up so high;
Will you rest upon my little bed?" said the Spider to the Fly.
"There are pretty curtains drawn around; the sheets are fine
       and thin,
And if you like to rest awhile, I'll snugly tuck you in!"
"Oh no, no," said the little Fly, "for I've often heard it said,
They never, never wake again, who sleep upon your bed!"

Said the cunning Spider to the Fly, "Dear friend what can I
       do,
To prove the warm affection I've always felt for you?

I have within my pantry, good store of all that's nice;
I'm sure you're very welcome – will you please to take a
      slice?"
"Oh no, no," said the little Fly, "kind sir, that cannot be,
I've heard what's in your pantry, and I do not wish to see!"

"Sweet creature!" said the Spider, "you're witty and you're
      wise,
How handsome are your gauzy wings, how brilliant are your
      eyes!
I have a little looking-glass upon my parlour shelf,
If you'll step in one moment, dear, you shall behold yourself."
"I thank you, gentle sir," she said, "for what you're pleased to
      say,
And bidding you good morning now, I'll call another day."

The Spider turned him round about, and went into his den,
For well he knew the silly Fly would soon come back again:
So he wove a subtle web, in a little corner sly,
And set his table ready, to dine upon the Fly.
Then he came out to his door again, and merrily did sing,
"Come hither, hither, pretty Fly, with the pearl and silver
      wing;
Your robes are green and purple – there's a crest upon your
      head;
Your eyes are like the diamond bright, but mine are dull as
      lead!"

Alas, alas! how very soon this silly little Fly,
Hearing his wily, flattering words, came slowly flitting by;
With buzzing wings she hung aloft, then near and nearer
      drew,

Thinking only of her brilliant eyes, and green and purple
        hue –
Thinking only of her crested head – poor foolish thing! At
        last,
Up jumped the cunning Spider, and fiercely held her fast.
He dragged her up his winding stair, into his dismal den
Within his little parlour – but she ne'er came out again!

And now dear little children, who may this story read,
To idle, silly, flattering words, I pray you ne'er give heed:
Unto an evil counsellor, close heart, and ear, and eye,
And take a lesson from this tale, of the Spider and the Fly.

Selected Early Modern Riddles

Anonymous

A riddle is a poem or phrase that contains a hidden clue to its meaning. These particular riddles were first published in 1916, but had already been around for hundreds of years previously. Their original authors would have spoken them aloud to entertain family and friends.

The answers are given below.

Higher than a house, higher than a tree;
Oh, whatever can that be?

*

Purple, yellow, red, and green,
The king cannot reach it nor the queen;
Nor can old Noll, whose power's so great:
Tell me this riddle while I count eight.

*

Two legs sat upon three legs,
With one leg in his lap;
In comes four legs,
And runs away with one leg.
Up jumps two legs,
Catches up three legs,
Throws it after four legs,
And makes him bring back one leg.

*

As round as an apple, as deep as a cup,
And all the king's horses can't pull it up.

*

As I went through the garden gap,
Who should I meet but Dick Red-cap!
A stick in his hand, a stone in his throat,
If you'll tell me this riddle, I'll give you a groat.

Answers:
a star
a rainbow
one leg is a leg of mutton; two legs, a man; three legs, a stool; four legs, a dog
a well
a cherry

My Shadow

Robert Louis Stevenson (1850–1894)

Robert Louis Stevenson originally wrote this poem for children who were afraid of the dark. Personification is used to give the shadow a character. In the final stanza, the shadow stays in bed. Can you explain why?

I have a little shadow that goes in and out with me,
And what can be the use of him is more than I can see.
He is very, very like me from the heels up to the head;
And I see him jump before me, when I jump into my bed.

The funniest thing about him is the way he likes to grow –
Not at all like proper children, which is always very slow;
For he sometimes shoots up taller like an India rubber ball,
And he sometimes gets so little that there's none of him at all.

He hasn't got a notion of how children ought to play,
And can only make a fool of me in every sort of way.
He stays so close beside me, he's a coward you can see;
I'd think shame to stick to nursie as that shadow sticks to me!

One morning, very early, before the sun was up,
I rose and found the shining dew on every buttercup;
But my lazy little shadow, like an arrant sleepy-head,
Had stayed at home behind me and was fast asleep in bed.

An Emerald Is as Green as Grass

Christina Rossetti (1830–1894)

Christina Rossetti published her first book of poetry when she was aged just 12. In this poem, she uses similes to describe the beauty of jewels. Look at the final line. What do you think the poem tells us about beauty?

An emerald is as green as grass;
　　A ruby red as blood;
A sapphire shines as blue as heaven;
　　A flint lies in the mud.

A diamond is a brilliant stone,
　　To catch the world's desire;
An opal holds a fiery spark;
　　But a flint holds fire.

Who Killed Cock Robin?

Traditional

"Who Killed Cock Robin" is a folk song, first published in full in around 1770. Some people think that the rhyme is about the death of Robin Hood, the legendary English outlaw. If this is so, why do you think the poet chose to represent the hero as a bird?

Who killed Cock Robin?
I, said the Sparrow,
with my bow and arrow,
I killed Cock Robin.

Who saw him die?
I, said the Fly,
with my little eye,
I saw him die.

Who caught his blood?
I, said the Fish,
with my little dish,
I caught his blood.
Who'll make the shroud?
I, said the Beetle,
with my thread and needle,
I'll make the shroud.

Who'll dig his grave?
I, said the Owl,
with my little trowel,
I'll dig his grave.

Who'll be the parson?
I, said the Rook,
with my little book,
I'll be the parson.

Who'll be the clerk?
I, said the Lark,
if it's not in the dark,
I'll be the clerk.

Who'll carry the link?
I, said the Linnet,
I'll fetch it in a minute,
I'll carry the link.

Who'll be chief mourner?
I, said the Dove,
I mourn for my love,
I'll be chief mourner.

Who'll carry the coffin?
I, said the Kite,
if it's not through the night,
I'll carry the coffin.

Who'll bear the pall?
We, said the Wren,
both the cock and the hen,
We'll bear the pall.

Who'll sing a psalm?
I, said the Thrush,
as she sat on a bush,
I'll sing a psalm.

Who'll toll the bell?
I said the Bull,
because I can pull,
I'll toll the bell.

All the birds of the air
fell a-sighing and a-sobbing,
when they heard the bell toll
for poor Cock Robin.

Time to Rise

Robert Louis Stevenson (1850–1894)

The bird in this four-line poem from Robert Louis Stevenson's collection *A Child's Garden of Verses* (1885) is very much alive. Notice how, in very few words, Stevenson manages to capture its quickness and vitality.

A birdie with a yellow bill
Hopped upon the window sill,
Cocked his shining eye and said:
"Ain't you 'shamed, you sleepy-head?"

A Riddle

Christina Rossetti (1830–1894)

This poem, from a collection called *Sing-Song*, published in 1872, takes the form of a riddle. Can you work out the answer?

> There is one that has a head without an eye,
> And there's one that has an eye without a head.
> You may find the answer if you try;
> And when all is said,
> Half the answer hangs upon a thread.

Selected Tongue Twisters

A tongue-twister is a phrase or short poem, often using alliteration and rhyme, and designed to be difficult to say. Try to say these examples quickly without tripping!

Peter Piper

Anonymous

Peter Piper picked a peck of pickled peppers.
A peck of pickled peppers Peter Piper picked.
If Peter Piper picked a peck of pickled peppers,
Where's the peck of pickled peppers that Peter Piper picked?

Betty Botta

Carolyn Wells (1862–1942)

Betty Botta bought some butter;
"But," said she, "this butter's bitter!
If I put it in my batter
It will make my batter bitter.
But a bit o' better butter
Will but make my batter better."
Then she bought a bit o' butter

Better than the bitter butter,
And she put it in her batter,
And it made her batter better.
So 'twas better Betty Botta
Bought a bit o' better butter.

You Know New York

Anonymous

You know New York.
You need New York.
You know you need unique New York.

GLOSSARY

Allegory – A poem is an allegory (or allegorical) if there is a hidden message, which is often moral.

Alliteration – Alliteration is the repetition of the same letter or sound at the beginning of words, such as "Betty Botta bought some butter".

Ballad – A ballad is a narrative poem which is usually sung. The stanzas typically have a simple structure, and there is often a chorus.

Blank verse – A poem which has no rhyming lines in it is described as being written in blank verse.

Couplet – A couplet is a pair of lines, which usually rhyme and have the same metre. Robert Louis Stevenson's "Happy Thought" is a single couplet.

Concrete poetry – Concrete poems are written in a particular shape.

Dialogue – A dialogue is a conversation between two or more characters. Speech marks are usually used to indicate dialogue.

Enjambement – Enjambement is where one line of a poem runs straight onto the next without any pause. An example can be found in "The Grey Squirrel" by Humbert Wolfe.

Form – The form of a poem is its structure. This includes details such as the number of lines, the rhythm of each line and the metre. The sonnet is a well-known poetic form.

Haiku – A haiku is a short three-line poem consisting of exactly 17 syllables: 5 in the first line, 7 in the second and 5 the third. The haiku originated in Japan, and was traditionally used to describe scenes from nature.

Imagery – Imagery is the use of descriptive words which help the reader to imagine particular sights, sounds, smells and feelings.

Limerick – A limerick is a humorous five-line poem which follows a particular rhyme and metre. Limericks are very distinctive, and usually start with a phrase such as "There was an old man from…".

Metaphor – A metaphor is used to compare two things. Whereas a simile is used to say that one thing is "like" another, a metaphor is used to suggest that one thing *is* another, because they share some important quality. In "Windy Nights", Robert Louis Stevenson uses the image of a highwayman as a metaphor for the sound of the wind at night.

Metre – Words are made up of stressed and unstressed syllables. For example, "book" is one stressed syllable and "paper" is a stressed syllable followed by an unstressed syllable. The pattern of these syllables in a line of a poem is called the metre.

Narrative poem – A narrative poem is one which tells a story.

Onomatopoeia – When a word is onomatopoeic, it sounds similar to the sound that is being described. Animal noises are often onomatopoeic, such as "oink!" or "meow!".

Personification – An object or animal is personified when it is described as having human actions or emotions.

Rhetorical question – A rhetorical question is a question which doesn't need an answer. Rhetorical questions are often used in poetry when the speaker wants to make a point about something.

Rhyme – Words rhyme when they are spelt differently, but sound similar. For example, "cow" rhymes with "now". The rhymes in poems often follow a pattern, known as a rhyme scheme. You can work out the rhyme scheme of a poem by writing a letter beside each line. Where the last word in the line rhymes with the last word in another line, they are given the same letter. In Christina Rossetti's poem "An Emerald Is as Green as Grass", the rhyme scheme is abcb:

An emerald is as green as grass,	a
A ruby red as blood;	b
A sapphire shines as blue as heaven;	c
A flint lies in the mud.	b

Rhythm – The rhythm of a poem is its beat, which is created from patterns of words and sounds as well as the metre of the poem.

Simile – A simile, like a metaphor, is used to compare two things. The words "like" or "as" are often used to make the comparison.

Sonnet – A sonnet is a 14-line rhyming poem which contains 10 syllables on each line. The last two lines of a sonnet are usually a rhyming couplet.

Stanza – Poems are often divided into stanzas, or sections, each of which has the same number of lines.

Subject – The subject is the character or thing that is being described in a poem.

Syntax – Syntax is the word order within a poem. Poets sometimes introduce unusual word order to create a particular emphasis.

NOTE TO TEACHERS AND PARENTS

Promoting the enjoyment and understanding of poetry is an important part of the National Curriculum for English at Key Stages 1 and 2. The poems in this collection feature a broad range of themes and techniques. Along with the accompanying discussion points, they support readers in developing the following skills:

- extending vocabulary
- identifying themes and conventions
- recognizing different poetic forms
- interpreting meaning
- evaluating use of language, including figurative language
- recognizing literary language and devices
- exploring structure and its effect on meaning
- expressing preferences.

INDEX OF TITLES AND AUTHORS

INDEX OF FIRST LINES